THE WONDERFUL WORLD OF

Disney

ANIMALS

by WILLIAM R. KOEHLER
Disney's Chief Animal Trainer for 21 Years

HOWELL BOOK HOUSE INC.
PUBLISHERS • NEW YORK

Library of Congress Cataloging in Publication Data

Koehler, William R

    The wonderful world of Disney animals.

    SUMMARY: Presents a behind-the-scenes account of
the techniques and trials of training various
animals who have appeared in Disney productions.
    1. Animals in moving-pictures.   2. Moving-
pictures—Plots, themes, etc.   3. Disney (Walt)
Productions.   [1. Animals in motion pictures.
2. Animals—Training]   I. Disney (Walt)
Productions.   II. Title.
PN1995.9.A5K6   636.08′88   79-12333
ISBN 0-87605-810-1

Contents

Foreword   9

Introduction   11

"Cute" Won't Make A Career   13

The Disney College Campus   16

The Shaggy Dog   21
  Hairy Hotrodder   29
  Sam Swims and Shares   35

Toby Tyler   39
  The Elephant Dogs of Toby Tyler   43

Swiss Family Robinson   47
  Rocky Trains the Trainer   51
  The Flying Animal Ark   54
  Treading Water   57
  Chatto Becomes a Jockey   66

Big Red   73
  Red Crashes Through a Window   79
  A Rare Kind of Dog Temperament   83
  How Red Was "Rigged" for a Weak, Wobbly Gait   87

The Incredible Journey   91
  "Warm and Real" Affection Between Dog and Cat   94
  Stream-Crossing Siamese   99
  Cool Cat and Hot Sand   103
  A Slick Scene   107

The Incredible Journey
With Six Animals, You Need Luck — 111
Syn and the Other Siamese Become Ill — 117

Bristle Face — 126
The Amateur Beats the Professionals — 128

Boomerang, Dog of Many Talents — 133
Prince and Tiger Handle a Hard-Headed Herd — 135
Compie's Cool Turkeys — 138

Those Calloways — 143
Short Haired Prince and Tiger in Snow and Sub-Zero Cold — 147
It's a Long Way to a Wolverine's Heart — 157

That Darn Cat — 163
"A Cat's in Business for Himself"—True or False? — 169
D. C. Eludes the F. B. I. Agents — 177
Teaching D. C. to Zero in on a Hidden Sound — 181

Charlie, the Lonesome Cougar — 185
"What do you want?" Quoth the Raven — 187

Sancho, the Homing Steer — 191
How to "Break" a Steer for Riding — 195
Getting the Fowls to Roost in Broad Daylight — 200

The Bears and I — 203
Ron Brown Finds a Picture — 207
Bear Love — 213

King of the Grizzlies — 217
Herding the Bears Up the Snow-clad Mountain — 220

The Ugly Dachshund — 225
The Dachsie Demolition Team — 231

The Olympic Game Farm — 243
The paradise where Disney animals go between the acts

To the memory of
Halleck (Hal) Driscoll,
my partner and true friend

Red knows he has three admirers.

Foreword

WILLIAM KOEHLER'S brilliant career as teacher, trainer and friend of animals spans more than three decades. It was in his capacity as Chief Trainer for the Walt Disney Studios that his singular talents came to national attention. For it was he who trained the "stars" of *Big Red, The Shaggy Dog, The Ugly Dachshund, The Incredible Journey* and many other celebrated animal actors. Five Koehler pupils won the American Humane Association's coveted "Patsy" awards for outstanding animal performances in motion pictures and television.

During World War II Mr. Koehler was an instructor in the U.S. Army's K-9 Corps. Since the War he held the post of Training Director for the Orange Empire Dog Club, the largest dog club in the world. The success of his methods with tens of thousands of happy, well-adjusted dogs offers testimonial to his remarkable ability. He has conducted clinics in dog training throughout the United States and Canada and, most recently, in South Africa.

His other book credits include *The Koehler Method of Dog Training, The Koehler Method of Guard Dog Training, The Koehler Method of Open Dog Training for Ring, Home and Field*, and *The Koehler Method of Utility Dog Training*. His work on Guard Dogs was named Best Dog Book of the Year of 1967 by the Dog Writers' Association of America.

In this marvelous book Bill Koehler reveals the love and patience, ingenuity and skill, and understanding of animal behavior and instinct that trainers of wild and domestic creatures must possess to achieve perfect performance on the screen. Finding the ideal specimen of its species to fit the requirements of the story or script is the trainer's first, and often frustrating, challenge. Then comes the seemingly impossible task of cueing the creature to do what does *not* come naturally to it (such as getting a wily and wicked wolverine to interact with a man!) Surprising, to some readers perhaps, will be the fact that the remarkable feats shown in the films involved no "trick" camera shots. And, as the last chapter fully testifies, the animals enjoy the tender care, kindness and respect of all Disney personnel. Walt himself would have it no other way.

This truly behind-the-scenes account of the techniques and trials of teaching all sorts of animals to act is a heartwarming Disney story all its own. Mr. Koehler writes it with charm, humor and wit. He pays tribute to Walt Disney, who took an affectionate and lively interest in his animal actors, and to the Disney directors, producers, photographers, human stars, and Bill's fellow trainers, whose support and cooperation contributed so much to the success of his own work.

The real-life heroes of this book are "Big Red," the Irish Setter; Syn, the Siamese cat in *The Incredible Journey;* Joey, the wolverine; Prince and Tiger, the Boxer-Redbone Hound crossbreds; Sam, the Shaggy Dog; and many other Disney animal characters who have brought so much joy to millions of movie fans all around the world through the magic of Walt Disney and the skills of Bill Koehler and his trainer-friends.

10

Introduction

WALT DISNEY gave fans two kinds of animal pictures; both of which did more than entertain.

One kind is the pure, unplotted, true-life film, such as *The Living Desert.* For these productions the studio hires individuals or teams, who are qualified as patient naturalists with great skill as cinema photographers, to go into an area and photograph a subject's actions in any order they occur until nature provides them with material which, when shown in proper sequence, will be a true-life drama.

True-life films have taught millions of viewers where and how some of the world's fascinating creatures live.

The second kind of Disney animal picture is plotted and staged in order to tell a story, whether the animals interact with other creatures or merely struggle against an environment.

These story pictures feature animals that are trained, or tamed, so that they can be made to act predictably at an appropriate time. They are handled by experienced trainers who can interpret a script in terms of the requirements and challenges that its story will impose on animals. The trainers select and prepare suitable animals to perform reliably in situations that are filled with many distractions. In addition to producing entertainment, the work of preparing animals for this kind of motion picture has yielded knowledge of temperament and training that would never have been gained were it not for problems encountered in the work. What laboratory-oriented research could create situations and experiments to match those structured for *The Swiss Family Robinson* and *That Darn Cat?*

It was the author's good fortune to be involved in most of the fine Disney animal pictures and to acquire some knowledge that could not be gained through ordinary association with animals nor within the constrictions of formal laboratory controls.

Walt Disney had an incisive way of "entrusting" us with problems. It is good to know that by solving those problems we are bringing you wholesome and unusual family entertainment. It should be equally satisfying for you to know that your approval of our pictures made it possible to create the situations from which we learned some widely useful things about animals. Thank you.

I hope this book will give you some more closeups of the Disney Animals you love.

William Koehler

"Cute" Won't Make a Career

THERE WAS a happy sound of stirring feet and thumping tails in aluminum crates as I turned our van into the long drive at Seeing Eye, near Morristown, New Jersey. Within a few days the comfortable kennels which had been provided for our dogs during Walt Disney's filming of *Atta Girl Kelley* had become a second home to them. I parked the van close to the kennel building; and Bob Harris, my assistant trainer, opened the door to the kennel's hallway and stood by as I opened the crates and each dog headed for his quarters and the exercise and food that would soon be coming. We cared for our dogs, made a final check and headed the van for our motel at Whippany, about fifteen miles from Seeing Eye.

The sun was low and the air channeling into the van felt good on our wet faces as we checked off the scenes we had completed in downtown Morristown. Bob read the call sheet that indicated the scene numbers and planning needed for the next day. He put the sheet away as we turned onto the freeway on our final mile to the motel, then leaned back in his seat and chuckled as he shook his head disbelievingly.

"Think you'll have another phone call?"

"Don't mention it," I answered.

I parked the van near our rooms, and we walked back to the office to check our boxes for mail.

"Bill, you've got a long distance call," one of our company said as we met at the office door.

"Oh, Mr. Koehler." One of the motel staff handed me a slip of paper. "Call this operator in Portland, Oregon."

There were two envelopes in my box. One of them was thick and heavy and marked "Photos."

Finally, in the coolness of my room, I pulled off my shoes, but I didn't relax. I opened the thick envelope and started shuffling through the pictures. It was no surprise that they were all of a Seal-point Siamese cat in a variety of poses. And it was no surprise, rather inevitable, that one featured the cat on the toilet seat of a fashionable bathroom.

The cat's authentic posture and obvious concentration showed it to be a candid shot. It was another one for my collection. I put the pictures back in the envelope, checked the number on the slip the clerk had given me, and placed my call to the Portland operator.

Too soon, I was listening to an enthusiastic owner tell me about her Siamese cat. Her voice dropped modestly. "Guess what she uses instead of a sandbox?"

"Tell me," I said.

A pause suggested she had looked over her shoulder. The voice dropped to a sweet and intimate whisper. "Our own toilet—in the bathroom."

"Goodness," I blurted.

Furthermore, her "Helen" had other earmarks of elegance that could be perpetuated were she to be mated with a deserving cat of equal social graces—such as Walt Disney's cat, Syn. But more importantly, motherhood could be deferred in favor of a career. Helen's speciality was available for a picture.

I thanked her sincerely for her interest; and explained

that Helen's specialty, though fascinating, was not the stuff of which pictures are made.

Fatigue, the summer's heat, and two more proud owners of cats with their own way of doing their thing, plus some hay fever tablets made me creatively maudlin. I thought of a story line that would fiendishly confine a cat in a room full of priceless Oriental rugs, only to have him open a bathroom door and make it to the toilet on time; but rejected it as being contrived. And production logistics would be formidable. Camera crews are patient, but there are limits. To wait, rigid and ready, until a cat felt moved would be out of the question. Good trainers depend on a positive motivation to cause an animal to act. Cathartics are positive but unpredictable. Nor would any mechanical means give the timing that would justify a camera crew's readiness. It would be a very expensive 'no go.'

These pictures and calls are examples of the kind of response that regularly follows some of the Walt Disney animal pictures. They indicate the enthusiasm owners often have for their own animals and confusion as to how animals are selected and prepared for feature roles. It is this interest and enthusiasm of our viewers that has made the production of good animal pictures possible. We are grateful to all of you for your interest in our animal friends.

In this book we will tell you how some of our actors were discovered and prepared for pictures, and how the Disney animals are cared for and protected. We will take you into the world of "Production" where they worked.

The Disney College Campus

THE "LOT" of Walt Disney Productions is often referred to as a "college campus." Its contrast with the environment of other studios justifies that description. Walt's desire for cleanliness is constantly evident. Wherever it is practical to do so, trees and other kinds of vegetation are used to give a park-like atmosphere. Grassy areas surround the immaculate buildings on the north side of the lot. Various kinds of shops, staffed by top artisans, are located on the southeast quarter of the main lot. The sound stages are grouped on the southwest quarter. The space around them must provide access for trucks and other heavy equipment, but Walt's wishes for order and neatness is reflected in the appearance of the buildings and streets. Close to the stages stands the Production Building, with related offices covering the second floor. The ground floor houses offices and some of the storage facilities and work rooms for the Set Decorating Department. It is the area on the west side of this building where the first showing of the animal candidates for picture roles generally takes place. Another thing often occurs there: a phenomenon of sorts.

Ordinarily, there might be a truck at the building's loading dock or a man pushing a flat truck of hand props down the ramp at one end of the dock on their way to a stage, and one or two other individuals entering or leaving the building. At the time of an animal "showing," the number of persons with "business" in the area increases remarkably. In the words of Barney Rogers who has scheduled most of the showings: "I wonder how they all find out about it?"

In addition to the producer and director, it is reasonable to suppose that the assistant director and a few others would be concerned with comparing the animal candidates for a job. Others in the audience would rarely have a reason to come to the vicinity of Set Decorating. But now they had a reason— they liked animals.

I recall these showings whenever I am asked if the people at Walt Disney Productions really like animals. They want to know particularly, if Walt Disney had a personal interest in the animals he starred. They want to know many things about the animals they've met through the Disney pictures. They want to know how the animals are found, how they are trained and conditioned for production and what steps are taken for their comfort and welfare. They want to know how the animals are motivated to play their roles. There are many misconceptions about such things.

Neither the acting ability of an animal nor his cute trick routines are ever reasons for starting a production. Occasionally, after he has struck a responsive chord, an animal will furnish the incentive for a series or a sequel—but rarely. As is most often true of pictures that feature only humans, first comes the story, whether it is an original or an adaptation. When the screen treatment is sufficiently advanced, actors with images that are compatible with the environment and the story line will be considered. Producers and directors review an actor's previous work, listen to readings, and shoot tests before casting a role. An actor's expertise in juggling would not win him an important part. Nor would the most amusing tricks by an adorable little dog carry a picture. Nor would a cat's amazing use of a toilet.

Dog actors, more than any other creatures, must be cast with attention to time and place. Dean Jones, with the help of makeup and wardrobe, could be perfectly acceptable in a picture set in biblical times. An Airedale appearing in a Civil War period would be laughable. We spent hours in research before we were sure that the cropped ears of the Great Danes that were used in *The Swiss Family Robinson* were not an anachronism. To avoid anachronisms, mixed breeds are often used as atmosphere dogs, but in a feature role they pose a problem. They are hard to "double." This protection of being easy to double is one of the many advantages of a purebred dog. It is appreciated by producers and by dog trainers who know where the best purebreds with some basic obedience training can be found. If a purebred is right for a part, a selection of principal dogs and good doubles can be found.

A small number of companies in the Los Angeles and New York areas provide qualified animals for picture production and commercials. Each of the companies has a stable of dogs, mixed breed and purebred, that work a lot in minor roles, but it requires more than this. When my partner and I prepared to show a specific breed for one of the Disney pictures, we turned first to the rosters of my large obedience class program. We looked for dogs that had graduated with high scores as evidence of trainability and emotional stability. Even novice obedience would give us a means of communication that would make a dog promptly feel comfortable with us. Open obedience for Companion Dog Excellent training would of itself provide ways of positively motivating a dog in many picture requirements. A dog that will, in addition to performing other exercises, retrieve a dumbbell in the obedience ring can be taught to lead a horse, grab an arm, or fetch anything reasonable with good timing. *The Shaggy Dog, Big Red, Sounder, Duke* and others are examples of dogs that would run to retrieve anything from a tin pan to a pirate.

Even though a first showing is often used only to compare type and character, it's easier to present a dog that will "do something" than one who can only stand. Though the producer and director might have "character" first in mind, they are certain to be impressed by evidence of trainability.

Often, if no decision is reached at the first showing, the trainers involved will be asked to give the most likely candidates some training on a significant character part and to bring the dog back for another showing. After a second or third showing, the dog chosen, with his trainer, will begin pre-production training. Walt Disney's generous investment in pre-production training has values that go beyond the production of superior animal pictures. The time and facilities provided make possible work that has illuminated many interesting facts on animal behavior. These facts could not have been learned in an experimental psychology laboratory.

"Don't tell me about the problems—I make the problems," Walt Disney told us all on many occasions.

Thank you, Walt, for making all those problems. We learned much.

The Shaggy Dog

The Film's Story

This delightful fantasy recounts the adventures of a teen-age boy who turns himself by magic into a sheep dog. It is loosely based on a touching novel by Felix Salten who wrote *Bambi.*

Young Wilby Daniels, played by Tommy Kirk, is the teen-ager who has fashioned his own make-shift science lab in the basement of his parents' small town home. He is always getting into trouble with his experiments. On one occasion, to the consternation of his mom (Jean Hagen) and dad (Fred MacMurray), Wilby almost blows up the house with a model rocket ship.

Allison (Annette Funicello), a young neighbor girl whom Wilby would like to date, thinks he is too immature for her and

It's so hard to understand why your brother turned into a dog.

It is not easy for a boy in a dog's body to gargle.

dates Wilby's friend Buzz Miller (Tim Considine). But when a new girl, Franceska (Roberta Shore), moves into the neighborhood with her father, one Dr. Andrassy (Alexander Scourby), recently appointed curator of the local museum, the two boys fall all over each other trying to impress her. Franceska, however, seems to have love only for her big, shaggy sheep dog named Chiffon.

Together the two boys escort Franceska to the museum where she and Buzz ditch Wilby amid the halls of statues. For company, Wilby talks to Professor Plumcutt (Cecil Kellaway), who is arranging an exhibit on sorcery. As the boy leaves, he accidentally spills a tray of antique rings.

That night Wilby finds a ring in a cuff of his trousers. Curiously he repeats aloud the Latin inscription on it and is gradually changed into Chiffon, the shaggy dog across the street.

Panic-stricken, he streaks for the museum on all fours and asks Plumcutt what he should do. The professor tells him simply that sometimes magic spells come and go like headaches and this one may just wear itself out.

Next morning, still a dog, Wilby reveals his plight to his brother Moochie (Kevin Corcoran), who is delighted to have a dog in the family, even if it is his brother. But, when discovered by his father, a mailman who hates dogs, Wilby has to flee for his life, and takes refuge with Franceska, who, of course, mistakes him for her own Chiffon.

While in the neighbor's house he discovers that the girl's father is planning to steal something from the local missile plant. The shaggy dog tries to get a look at the plans and makes such a pest of himself that Stefano, the butler (Jacques Aubuchon), locks him in a closet. There, the pooch turns back into teen-ager Wilby, who escapes.

As a dog, Tommy knocks his rival Tim down.

It's time for a bit of detective work.

The following evening, Wilby and Buzz go to the country club dance with Allison and Franceska. Wilby is blissfully dancing with Franceska when he begins changing back into her dog. He scrams before she notices and again takes refuge at Franceska's house — as Chiffon.

This time Wilby, the dog, overhears the spies as they plan their getaway. It is late the next day before he can get out of the house, tell his brother, and try to reveal the plot to his father. Mr. Daniels, however, keels over when he hears Wilby's voice coming from a dog. The police refuse to believe Moochie's tale about spies, and Wilby is trying to decide what to do next when Stefano, the butler, collars "Chiffon" and hauls him back to the old mansion.

When Moochie finally convinces his father that Wilby has actually turned into a dog and that the spy story is true, Daniels goes to the missile plant and repeats the story to security officers, who think him psychopathic.

Once again spying on the spies, the shaggy Wilby learns that Franceska knows nothing about their villainy and is not even Andrassy's true daughter. But, as fate would have it, he changes back to his old self while sitting there listening and is discovered. Stefano ties him up and locks him in a dressing room. The spies then take the protesting Franceska with them and speed for the waterfront.

Wilby changes back to a dog and frees himself just as Moochie shows up to help. When the unsuspecting Buzz arrives in his hot rod to take Franceska on a date, the shaggy dog comes bounding out of the house, bowls him over, commandeers the souped-up jalopy and speeds after the spies. Not believing their eyes, two amazed policemen give chase in their prowl car as Mr. Daniels, released by security at the missile plant, follows suit.

A boy in a dog's body finds it hard to arrange an escape.

Give me the police.

To the rescue!

The Shaggy Dog

At the waterfront, Shaggy is just in time to make a pier-head leap upon the spies as they take off in a speedboat. In the ensuing melee, Franceska is pushed overboard. Shaggy Wilby quits the fight to rescue her. As the half-drowned girl regains her senses, Wilby changes to his normal appearance and Chiffon suddenly materializes on the scene. The spies are picked up by the harbor patrol and Franceska naturally thinks her pet is a hero. And so does everyone else when the story hits the papers. But Wilby leaves well enough alone and says nothing of his part in the capture. After all, who would believe him?

The Training

The lovable clown cast in the title role of *The Shaggy Dog* is an Old English Sheepdog of champion parentage. He was not a trick dog and took on the role after only thirty days of obedience training. Bill Koehler says Shaggy was a "method" actor and in the following accounts tells us how he trained the dog to "drive" the souped-up hot rod and to save Franceska from drowning.

Hairy Hotrodder

LILLYBRAD'S SAMMY'S SHADOW made his first public appearance in an obedience class I was running in San Bernardino. He porpoised into the first class as though he was two thirds of the way through a countdown that could launch him straight up in the air or on a good will tour of the other dogs and people who froze to watch him. He was convinced that he was something more than "just another dog." It was easy to see why Billye Anderson, Sam's mistress, had started him in serious training at four months. His dynamics channeled and controlled, Sam scored high in a graduation that required him to do all the novice obedience exercises after only nine weeks of training.

I remember telling Billye Anderson: "If there's ever a good picture job for a Sheepdog, I'd like to borrow him."

The picture came a year later. My partner, Hal Driscoll, learned that Walt Disney Productions had viewed more than twenty Old English Sheepdogs for the title role in a picture to be called *The Shaggy Dog*. Each of them had exhibited the contemporary curse of the breed: degrees of neurosis that varied from "geared and dingy" to cowardly and emotionally unstable. It appeared that the dearth of qualified candidates would set the stage for Sam who qualified in temperament and had novice obedience training.

29

"Call Barney Rogers and tell him about that Sheepdog you had in a class," Hal said in an early morning phone conversation.

Barney Rogers, as part of his wide spectrum of responsibility for the set decorating department, arranged the animal showings for Walt Disney Productions.

I called Barney and bluntly asked: "How would you like to see a good Sheepdog?"

It might have been my confident tone as well as my description that convinced him that Sam was worth seeing.

"Let me see when we can set up a showing."

"Let Hal know," I told him. "I think I can arrange to have Sam in town, so Hal can get him down there in a hurry."

Prayerfully, I called Mrs. Anderson. She graciously agreed to my proposal that her beloved Sam stay with Hal so that he would be ready for a showing on short notice.

Our firm of Allied Movie Dogs operated out of two kennels. The location that Hal and his wife Peggy maintained was located in the San Fernando Valley, quite convenient to the production studios. It was there that we had our office and kennels for dogs that worked often in small parts. Our other location, at Ontario, was ideally situated for training. It was close to the distracting sights and sounds of industry and agriculture that are needed to prepare a dog for the stresses of a motion picture role.

On the morning following my conversation with Barney Rogers, I took the beautifully groomed Sam in to meet Hal and to wait for the showing. As always, Sam owned all the ground he walked on; and Hal's Irish grin got wider and wider as Sam performed all of the basic obedience exercises. When I left them standing together on the drive, Sam looked as if he'd staked his claim to a new part of the world, and Hal was grinning as if he owned the only shillelagh in town.

A few days later Hal phoned me. "They liked him—all of them. They want to see him again."

"Again" was about a week later. Hal called me from a pay phone at the studio. "Sam sold himself. They gave me the script. I'll bring him back out there so you can get started. They want to put you both on pre-production salary."

"The script!" It seemed that, in addition to promising top entertainment, Bill Walsh and Lillie Hayward, the writers, had programmed an exhaustive temperament test for the dog. Driving a hot rod. Doing an attack scene while draped with a fish net. Diving into the water. Part of the time Sam would be playing the part of a boy.

Goethe said, "Boldness has genius, power and magic in it." We began the test.

The driver's position in the hot rod would demand that Sam must sit on a bucket seat with his front feet in correct position on the steering wheel. He must be conditioned to many angles of motion, to the rush of wind, and to the sound of the motor and travel noises. It would be different than the car rides that most dogs enjoy.

Sam's novice training would allow us to start some wheel-barrow conditioning immediately. I used rubber bands to hold the long hair from his eyes, and jumped him into a wheelbar-row. He had a solid sit-stay and readily accepted the strange-ness of the motionless wheelbarrow. After a minute, I released him and gave him lots of praise. He jumped out and shoved my leg with the side of his head, and, with his body bowed, managed to wag his rear in a way that said, "No matter how crazy you are, I trust you."

I interspersed sit-stays in the wheelbarrow with some breaks and other exercises until it seemed Sam was ready to be tried with his environment in motion. He sat steady like a sand bag as I wheeled him slowly along.

Within the next few days, Sam came to regard the wheelbarrow as a pleasant means of transportation. Pavement, bumpy ground, varied speeds, steep grades and tight circles were all the same to him. He faced ahead like a hairy helmsman. It was time for the next level.

As said before, Walt Disney Productions offered, in addition to the environment of the sound stages, almost unlimited facilities for the emotional conditioning of a dog. A particularly useful bit of equipment is the "flat," a four wheel platform with a rail at each end to secure a lead and to provide a comfortable grip for pushing heavy items from the Set Decorating Department to the stages. The swivel wheels permit a maneuverability making the flat ideal for the next level of Sam's conditioning. The rail on the "bow end" would give him practice in holding a "feet up" as he would have to do on the wheel of the hot rod.

Sam had already learned to do a "feet up," a picture exercise that requires a dog to rear up and place his front feet on a designated spot. With an agility that always surprised, Sam bounced onto the flat and arched his pasterns over the rail. It was another adventure and he was for it. I pushed him on a "Cook's tour" around the lot and from the bright sunlight into the gloom of an unlighted stage. The daily tours, with the big dog skilfully balancing against bumps and turns brought only smiles from the studio personnel who were appreciative but not surprised by any creatures, whether living, mechanical or drawn. But often a stranger to the lot appeared to wonder if there might really be an Oz.

"Tours" and other work were sometimes interrupted by calls to go to Special Effects for a "fitting." The hot rod was being modified and equipped for Sam's security and comfort. A bucket seat had been carefully contoured to his ample sheepdog rear and placed conveniently. For his stability and absolute safety there were mittens to make it easy for him to hold his front feet on the wheel and a seatbelt to prevent him from sliding. Mittens and belt were covered with hair that would blend perfectly with Sam's own shimmering coat.

"Let's see what he thinks of it," a special effects man said.

Sam relaxed and watched quizzically while we laced the mittens over his feet. On the command, "Feet up," he placed his paws on the only obvious thing before him—the wheel. Meticulously integrated thongs anchored the mittens in the steering position. On the other side of the car, a man stooped to reach another wheel which was concealed, with other controls, for the use of a "blind driver" who would drive the car while aligned, prone and invisible, with a viewing slot. The two steering wheels were sychronized with sprockets and a cycle chain. When the blind driver's wheel was turned, Sam's wheel and his feet would match every movement. Whether his feet moved the wheel or the wheel moved his feet would not be apparent unless he offered resistance.

There was a wave of laughter as we all watched a perfect illusion. Sam offered no resistance nor the slightest concern. There was only cooperation and participation that made the illusion of driving perfect.

Neither did rocking the car nor pushing it back and forth seem to bother Sam.

Bill Walsh, Walt's Associate Producer on the picture, was one of those who had watched Sam pass the test of the car. "Sam just seems to go along with everything."

Bill's comment described Sam's attitude nicely. We knew with that attitude going for us, we would solve the problem of the car. Now we could introduce Sam to some of the other strange situations.

The Shaggy Dog borrows a car.

Sam Swims and Shares

DIVING AND SWIMMING were two things that Sam would have to do in a life saving scene. Because he would have to portray the right attitude as well as the action, we would have to introduce him to water carefully. He must be heroic. There could be no inhibitions.

"We'll have to make him want to go in," I told Frank Driscoll, who would work with me on the picture.

A half hour later we were walking along one of the few flatland creeks in our area. When the creek narrowed a bit, I waded across. With Frank and Sam on the opposite side we worked our way along to where the creek was slightly wider and about a foot deep. I uncoiled my longe line and threw the snap end across to Frank. He fastened it to Sam's collar, and then moved away. After a couple of attempts to follow Frank, Sam sat down and looked to where I held the other end of the line. He moved down to the edge of the water and sat down again.

I gave a recall command. Sam wanted none of it. He moved along the bank upstream without finding a dry place to cross. Then he probed his way back downstream as far as the line would allow. He moved back to a location directly across from me. He put one hairy foot gingerly out on the water and jerked it back. His head went up and down as he looked alternately from the wet barrier before him to where I was standing. Hair hid his expression, but I had a hunch that a little more pressure might get him to enter the water. I looped the end of the longe around a small willow that grew near the bank, and walked directly away from the creek, and looked over my shoulder. Sam was again moving back and forth on the bank. Finally he chose the only route to me—through the water. He crossed the creek with a martyr's tread and came out with his heavily coated legs a third of their usual diameter. He responded to my praise with the usual hard root of his muzzle.

"Let's move up a bit farther," I said to Frank. "I want the water a little deeper, but not too deep. It could give him a setback if he went under."

Frank and I changed sides, and he held the longe while Sam watched my crossing. This time, Sam hardly hesitated to cross as he saw me walk away from the bank.

"Let's move up again," I told Frank.

Once more we changed sides of the stream and Frank held Sam as we worked our way up to where a pool appeared to be about right for Sam's next experience.

"This is it," I called across to where Frank stood with the big dog. "If we move up any farther, he'll go under."

Frank threw the line toward me. As though the motion were a signal, Sam lunged like a hairy dolphin into the water shoulder deep. Another lunge changed his direction toward a deeper part of the pool. He plunged from sight. He boiled to the surface, sleek as a seal and angled across the pool with the instinctive paddling of a dog who hasn't had enough practice to settle into the water. He made it to shore and shook himself as only an Old English Sheepdog in full coat can shake. No smoothly contoured sheets of water as from another breed, rather, great predictable plumes flung several yards by the long gray hair.

Frank and I froze to watch for the effect of his experience. Would he feel that the wet world wasn't to be trusted? How long would it take to rebuild his confidence to get the attitude we needed?

Suddenly Sam turned and lunged back in Frank's general direction. Again, his second lunge left him with water above and below him. He came out, plodded up the bank, and shook mightily. He faced around toward me and sat down triumphantly in the heat of the day. The expression on his wet face was very apparent. One lip was caught between his teeth. He cocked his head thoughtfully as though wondering whether I knew the joys of being wet. Sam had discovered water.

Mr. Stubbs terrifies all the bystanders when he seizes the sheriff's gun.

Mr. Stubbs expresses his shame and gives Kevin the gun.

Toby Tyler

The Film's Story

This Disney production of James Otis's ever popular tale fulfills in Technicolor nearly every small boy's dreams of running away from home and joining a circus.

Among the cast of human and animal performers, including the gun-toting chimpanzee "Mr. Stubbs," are the clowns' dogs of mixed breeds.

The Training

In the next account Mr. Koehler reveals how he and his fellow trainers got the dogs to don elephant costumes and how the problem of "chicken hypnosis" was solved.

Mr. Stubbs surprises the strong man with a feat of strength.

Clown makes boy and four dogs happy when
he tells them Mr. Stubbs will recover.

The clown's four dogs line up to be fed.

Toby Tyler and Mr. Stubbs run away from the circus rather than be separated.

The Elephant Dogs
of *Toby Tyler*

A MOTION PICTURE TRAINER learns things about animals that would never be observed in other environments. For example, in what other situations would a trainer be asked to teach dogs to wear elephant costumes and parade single file, trunk-to-tail? This was one of the acts that the clown's dogs were supposed to perform in *Toby Tyler*.

First of all came lots of careful measuring by our Special Effects Department. The five dogs graduated downward from a medium size to the very small one who was last in line, and there were great differences in head and body types. In between fittings, we worked the dogs in harnesses that were linked together with wood shafts so that they would become accustomed to the positions and speed of the parade order.

When all five costumes fitted to perfection, we took our dogs to stage four to see how they looked in the link-up. Again, Special Effects had created something that was truly art. Except for size, the latex costumes appeared real to sight. Each elephant head was molded smoothly into the body shell and tail assembly, regardless of each dog's size and form. A traditional ornamental star was cut in the center of each forehead. A narrow vertical bar of the material was left in the middle of

the star to strengthen the forehead. We three trainers and the man from Special Effects took one last look through each of the heads from the dog's point of view. It appeared that the vision through the eyeholes would be adequate.

Many fittings had conditioned the dogs to their costumes and they stood, tails wagging and responsive to the attention, while their heads and body skirtings were fastened. We placed them in their planned order. "Ginger," the tallest, would be led by Gene Sheldon who was cast as the clown and master of the dog act. Each of the others, in stepped down order, would get direction through his "trunk" which was attached to the costume tail of the dog in front of him.

"Great—they look great," said Charles Barton, the Director. "Now let's see them move."

Cindy James took the end of the prop leash and gave a command. Ginger started forward and, as their trunks barely tightened, each dog followed. Then the procession stopped as though from an airbrake system. "Mouse" fell over on his side and laid very quiet. "Rags" was next to topple. Within seconds our entire parade was lying on its side and askew.

We trainers rushed in and took the costumes from the dogs. Before a word broke the silence, the heads started to rise from the floor. There was a "Where-have-I-been" look on each face. Then, almost in unison, the dogs were standing firmly on their feet. They showed no ill effects from their experience.

"It's like they were anesthetized," someone said.

"No—not the way they came out of it," a voice argued. "It's more like they were hypnotized."

Hypnosis! It did appear that they all "went under" when the procession started to move. And they came out of it suddenly, as though from a trance. But how did motion cause the hypnosis? I knew that animals can be placed in a trance by unusual conditions, or a forced focus, as when a chicken is placed with its eyes faced to a line drawn on a pavement. But our dogs had no line. Or did they?

On a hunch I picked up a mask and put it to my face. If a dog looked through the eye holes, there was no line. But if he chose to look through the star, there was the bar in the middle. Right in the middle of his focus as he moved along would be an endless line. Others of our group knew of the "chicken hypnosis" principle.

It took only a few minutes for a workman to snip out the bars.

We put the costumes back on the dogs and re-established the line. No dog seemed stressed or even suspicious.

Once more we started our parade across the big sound stage. Ten feet. Twenty feet. No stops. No falls. There were mixed sighs of relief and cheers as our "elephants" paraded across the stage in the best circus tradition.

Swiss
Family Robinson

The Film's Story

Walt Disney went to the fragrant, palm-studded isle of Tobago — once a desert island in its own right — to film this exciting and widely read adventure story by Johann Wyss. The picture became one of Disney's all-time box office hits.

Disney chose a star-studded cast for the Swiss Family: among them, the Father, noted British actor John Mills; the Mother, Dorothy Maguire who starred in such great films as *Three Coins in a Fountain* and *A Tree Grows in Brooklyn;* the eldest son Fritz, James MacArthur whose real-life mother is Helen Hayes and who himself plays in the popular TV series *Hawaii Five-O;* the two younger sons Ernst and Francis, acted by Tommy Kirk and Kevin Corcoran who took the parts of Wilby and Moochie in *The Shaggy Dog;* Roberta, played by England's pretty "Miss Television," Janet Munro; and the sinister pirate chief, portrayed by Sessue Hayakawa who was the scheming Japanese colonel in *Bridge on the River Kwai.*

Fleeing from the oppression of Napoleon, the Swiss Family from Berne is stranded on a desert island after pirates chase their ship into a storm and disaster on offshore rocks. The family gets safely to land in a makeshift tubraft and later salvages supplies, domestic animals and firearms from the wreck. They build a fabulous treehouse for their comfort and a unique fortress for protection against the pirates, who return to search for Roberta. She has been snatched from their grasp by Fritz and Ernst during exploration of the island. Sustained action, laughter and a charming love story keep the plot moving at high speed to a totally unexpected climax.

Though Tobago was well populated with native animal life, Disney — to provide the kaleidoscopic zoological scene dreamed up by the author of the book — airlifted tigers, hyenas, ostriches, zebras, a baby elephant, cheetahs, huge lizards, giant snakes, monkeys and nearly a hundred exotic birds to the island and out again.

The Training

Bill Koehler describes now the huge logistic problems of loading and landing this flying "Noah's Ark" — and how they were safely solved without loss or injury to the animals. Following this successful feat Bill relates how he and his son got the Family's pet Great Danes, Turk and Duke, to swim through the treacherous waters from the wrecked ship to the raft — without visible human-trainer aid. The third animal segment covered by Bill from *The Swiss Family Robinson* involves the difficult task of having Chatto, the Panamanian Spider monkey, ride on Duke's back, another mission accomplished without human participation before the camera!

The sea calms and the animals make it to shore.

The porker barreled ashore.

No wet feathers on these chickens!

Kevin loans his elephant for launching an outrigger.

Rocky Trains the Trainer

WE WERE a few thousand feet above the sparkling Caribbean when the elephant's trunk reached out to touch Wes, our reptile man, gently on the cheek. Wes was sleeping soundly, slumped forward on the bench seat of our C-46 cargo plane. There had been long, hot hours of loading our animals, and our takeoff from New Orleans to Tobago seemed to be the signal to arrange our bones and muscles among our animals for some rest. The scraping of the wind on the plane's uninsulated skin was like a lullaby and all our crew was soon dozing.

We awoke a bit stiff, but cool and rested, and noticed a bright attitude on the part of our fellow creatures which showed that they had also relaxed. Rocky, our quarter-grown elephant, had not only relaxed, but in the way of her kind was checking our environment with her wonderfully facile trunk. One of the first things to intrigue her, as she reached between the bars of her cage, was Wes Dickenson's face.

I was fascinated by the variety of Wes's expressions, and wondered how long he could take it as the trunk's tip surveyed his ear, nose, mouth and closed eyelids. Without opening his eyes, Wes pushed the trunk away. "Quit it, Rocky," he said.

Rocky stood for a few moments as though savoring her find of something animate. Then the trunk reached out again.

Kevin's friend has a sweet tooth.

It began to retrace its first exploration. Its "finger" was at his chin when Wes opened his eyes and looked foolishly at his admirer. Then he reached into a sack that stood between the end of the bench and the bulkhead, and took one of the pieces of apple that had been cut up for the birds. Rocky's trunk stretched to receive the goody. Wes sighed and closed his eyes. If Wes sought to buy only a few seconds of relief, that's all he bought. Again the trunk came out. The pattern was about the same, but in rhythm and emphasis, more appreciative. Once more Wes stretched to the sack for a piece of apple. The trunk was ready.

I watched, wondering about Wes's long range planning, and saw the trunk start out again. This time, the pattern had barely started before Wes responded, with his eyes hardly open. This transaction took less time than the previous ones. Wes had gained no time for resting. How quickly he had turned a chance exploration into a lesson. And how quickly he had taught the elephant a routine. But somehow that didn't seem to be the bottom line. I had an uneasy feeling that I had come to the wrong conclusion.

I watched the trunk come out again. Its tip went to Wes's cheek and gave one little tap. It was definitely a cue. Only a cue. Wes responded. He leaned toward the bag. Now it was all very clear. Rocky had taught Wes to feed her apples.

The Flying Animal Ark

THE DOOR of our plane finally closed and the five of us wiped the sweat from our faces and looked around at our cargo. At last it was loaded and balanced. Our elephant was centered over the wing. Gertrude, our big pregnant Anaconda boa, a huge land tortoise, baggage and some of our smaller bird crates filled the space between the elephant's crate and the bulkhead. Space for feet and legs were left in front of a short seat bench that ran for ten feet along the portside beneath four small windows. Behind the wing section were some of our tigers, zebras, and a mule, and other heavy animals. Dozens of bird crates were arranged on top of the big carriers. Our six Great Danes thumped in their crates, with their noses to the doors to study the odors. Fenced off with crating material in the narrow space of the tail section, four of our ostriches were already cocking their heads and picking at rivets and other attractive things. We were as wet as if we had crawled from a pool. The loading had been a lot of work, even with fork lifts and other good equipment loaned to us by an airline.

"Now how do we unload this ark when we get to Tobago?" one of our crew asked.

Animal trainers are worriers. Our concern was not with how to save labor in unloading our animals, but how to do the job without risk of injury to them. The studio had sent George

Emerson, an experienced circus menagerie man, to Tobago earlier to supervise construction of animal quarters and a compound, but we supposed he would be limited as to cargo handling equipment.

Occasionally as we droned across the brilliant Gulf of Mexico and the Caribbean Sea, one of the crew would offer an idea on our problem, but none of the thoughts could relate until we saw the physical situation. We wondered if it would be pavement, rough ground or mud.

After a fuel stop and breakfast in Jamaica, we droned on for more hours. A tropical night pulled its blanket over the sea, and we felt the throttle setting and the plane's attitude change slightly. The landing gear rumbled down and the flaps braced against the air. The plane flared out, hung level for a few heavy seconds, then settled onto a surface that sent shudders from wheels to wing tips. A dirt strip — and we had hoped for a paved cargo ramp.

The plane finished its roll-out, and the engines stopped. All was quiet except for the hum of many voices against an orchestrated, primitive sound. There was no sound of power equipment.

The door of the plane opened to reveal hundreds of smiling faces. The wild sound increased in volume, and we identified it as the choral effort of thousands of tree frogs.

Then the juggernaut appeared. It was a huge ramp, lined on each side by scores of husky workmen who pushed it out of the crowd and, with little effort, across the moist earth to rest tightly against the cargo sill of the plane.

The ramp was so long that its incline from plane to ground was slight. The pushers jumped onto their ramp and, reinforced by others from the crowd, swarmed into the plane and took hold of our cargo. The ant-like stream reversed its direction and our precious animals were borne safely down the giant ramp, then in various directions to trucks and low, heavy trailers. No professional freight crew bottle-necked behind conveyors and equipment could have matched the speed of unlimited manpower diffused by the big ramp.

What a beautiful principle! An eternal truth. In physical situations that are not completely predictable, many workers acting independently and intelligently will always be more effective than a force programmed by machines or computers.

None of us who watched individual initiative and effort move our animals down the big ramp would ever again wonder how the Chinese built their Great Wall.

Treading Water

WHEN TURK AND DUKE scrambled up the sloping deck and dove over the rail of the wrecked *Swallow* and cut the water far below, my son Dick and I thought our hardest water shot had been made. Then we analyzed another scene from the viewpoint of a camera that would be mounted on a rock ten feet above the nearest waves. A reef sloped from that high point straight out toward the open sea. Another reef ran parallel to it to form a channel about a hundred feet wide. At the seaward end of the reef more of the same dark colored combination of lava and coral angled out to sea like wings on a catch pen. It was these wings that caused the tides to roar through the channel with awesome force.

It was through this channel that the Swiss Family Robinson would guide their makeshift raft on the passage from the *Swallow* to land. It was in the channel that our dogs were supposed to overtake the raft and be pulled aboard. The problem would be to compose the shot, with the dogs starting in correct relationship to the raft so that the action would be acceptable to the camera. There is no way to put a dog on a stay while he is swimming in rough water and the handler is at a great distance. Even a retriever, when he is trying to raise himself high in the water, will move some as he treads water. If we were to place the dogs from boats, they would be out of

The first trip to shore is rough.

Turk and Duke can't wait to take off for land.

position before the boats could clear camera.

We watched from shore while the crew started to take the raft through the channel on a trial run. The currents had twisted the raft apart on previous trials, but the men who had reinforced it were confident their work would stand the test. That test came when the raft reached a point opposite the camera platform. A tub popped out of its place in the frame; then the waves rolled others from their places and set them drifting. Household items that the prop men had packed in and between the tubs were swept about on the surface. Unbelievably, opposing currents began to carry the items in all directions. There seemed to be no general direction to the movement of water; a fact we knew that could add to the difficulty of holding our dogs in a proper relationship.

The breakup of the raft caused the shot to be postponed until the raft could be revamped. Before we left the location, Dick and I went over the problems of the shot again. The major difficulty was still that of holding the dogs in position for the shot then getting the boats or swimmers out of the scene before the dogs got out of place.

Dick is a strong swimmer. He would handle Duke in the water. Peter Grant, a native of Tobago, was equally qualified, particularly in swimming below the surface where he had spent countless hours spearfishing. He would hold Turk in place for the start of the shot. It was the thought of Peter's underwater experience that suggested a wild chance to Dick. If he and Peter could hold the powerful dogs in place until the shot started and, at the moment of release, swim beneath the surface until they were clear of the sidelines or the shot had ended, we would have a chance. It was a slim chance, but the only hope we had for a complete scene.

On the following day, power boats plied erratic courses in

the channel as the crew prepared for the big shot. Personnel and camera equipment were moved gingerly from the boats to the big rock. The raft had been rebuilt, and a variety of household items again filled the tubs.

The raft was held in place against the currents by the idling motors of two boats manned by prop men. Because of the high camera angle and the fact that the family would be looking away from camera as they watched the abandoned dogs try to overtake the raft, doubles could be used in the shot. I would double for Dorothy McGuire, so that I could be on the raft to call the dogs with my whistle. I was supplied with a heavy wool dress and a wig.

When we were settled in our places on the raft, boats took the swimmers and dogs to their positions. Dick and Peter eased over the sides of their boats and treaded water while the boatmen handed the dogs over to them. The boats backed swiftly away, and I could see the swimmers twisting against the power of the big dogs and the pull of the currents. The dogs were finally faced directly toward the raft, about ten feet apart, and held by their heavy collars.

As I huddled in my tub, back to the camera and whistle in my mouth, I felt we were about to try one of the most unpredictable shots imaginable. How could we even guess at a swimmer's chances of holding his orientation until he reached the sidelines? How would distance and time register in a world of strange forces and no landmarks?

A bull horn hurled the voice of the assistant director above the sound of the wind and waves. The camera was rolling. We wanted every foot of film we could get and the editor could take out the part that showed the boys still on the surface. If they could both stay below that surface once they had submerged, we could have something.

Suddenly, where there had been human heads, there were black swim-fins, and then only surging water. I groaned around the whistle, as Duke turned about, obviously concerned with Dick's absence. He turned back toward the sound of my whistle, and when he came up out of a big trough he was swimming steadily beside Turk. I kept urging them with the whistle. Soon they had closed half the distance to the raft and it was easy to see their faces as they pumped herocially through the swells. If they could reach the raft before the swimmers surfaced, we would have the whole shot. The dogs rode another big swell, then came sliding down toward us. They dropped from sight behind the next swell, and then the pumping legs pulled them within a few feet of the raft. I wondered how close we were to camera and how the scene looked from there.

"Cut," blared the bullhorn. "We got the shot."

There was a wild cheer from all of us. Then silence as we saw no swimmers. There was no way they could hear the bullhorn. We could only wait until they were forced to surface. Then they broke water in unison. Each had made it through the snarling currents to his own sideline. They had protected the shot all the way.

Dick and Peter added their own victory signal to those they saw, then relaxed and waited for the boats to pick them up.

It had been an Olympic swim for men and dogs—under conditions that were far from Olympic.

Turk and Duke check out a new arrival to the beach.

Kevin finds his mount to be smooth but slippery.

The tiger watches Kevin.

Janet Munro's mount has its own racing stripes.

A vulture knows the zebra
is in trouble.

Tommy Kirk warms up his entry.

Kevin Corcoran and James MacArthur move their mounts into position for the race.

Chatto Becomes a Jockey

WALT DISNEY ranged widely in his capacity of "a bee." When we needed to know how much reliability could be expected of a spider monkey while he was working at liberty, Walt referred me to Dr. Palmer of the San Diego Zoo. Dr. Palmer's opinion of the creature's potential for work was not very favorable. He reminded me that even the organ grinder's monkey, generally a tractable capuchin, is worked on a chain in his simple routine of collecting coins. Never in his long association with animal trainers had he known anyone who could work a monkey at liberty with the reliability needed for motion pictures—particularly on the densely forested island where we would shoot *The Swiss Family Robinson*.

I thanked Dr. Palmer for probably saving us from wasted time, and turned to leave his office.

"Which way do you go home from here?" he called after me.

"Route 395," I told him.

"Then stop off in Escondido and talk to 'Monkey Bill.' He's done more with all kinds of monkeys than anyone else I know." I waited while he wrote an address and directions. "His place is easy to find, and only a couple of blocks off the highway."

Two hours later I stopped in front of Monkey Bill's house, hoping that he would be more optimistic than Dr. Palmer on the trainability of monkeys.

Monkey Bill was an elderly man, tall and impressive in his manner and movements. As a preface to any discussion, he took me to a building behind his house and ushered me into the presence of a Rhesus monkey who stood on a table. The monkey was dressed in cowboy garb. A toy revolver hung low on each hip. It was plain from his expression that "the cowboy" would have preferred real guns and the chance to use them. Suddenly, on a cue I didn't see, the gunslinger drew and lined the guns up with my middle. On another cue the guns clopped back into their holsters.

Bill handed me a baseball of official size and weight. "Toss it to him."

The rhesus made a nice two-handed catch. Then, both hands still on the ball, he threw it back to me in the way a basketball player snaps a two-handed pass from his chest. His performance, with his handler at a distance, brought hope to my heart and a question to my mind.

"Will he work for you outside without any kind of a line—completely at liberty as an animal does in a picture?"

"No," Bill said. "There's only one monkey you can trust at liberty. It's a wooley. And a wooley can't do much."

Further research in monkey behavior failed to unearth anyone who had trained monkeys to work reliably at liberty. And "liberty" in our case meant such things as riding on the back of a Great Dane amidst the tropical vegetation on the island of Tobago.

Tobago and liberty would come at a later date, but now we needed to accustom each of our dogs to the presence of a monkey on his back. Local sources offered a limited choice and we had to settle for the only one of a correct age that we could find. Until now, the monkey had been avoided more than handled, and it was quite a task to hold all those legs, body and tail as we measured him for a saddle. Our Special Effects Department designed and fitted a beautiful little saddle which our Danes demonstrated they would wear as casually as a collar. A monkey will use his hands to remove a collar, so we tied our unwilling jockey to the saddle with a hip-collar and a short cord. He jerked against the cord for awhile, then settled into the saddle and held his seat even when the dog trotted. But each time he was placed on a dog the little beast fought the line until convinced that he was solidly anchored. Obviously he was not one to trust at liberty.

By the time we were ready to obtain health certificates for the animals we would take to Tobago, we learned that we would pick up forty Panamanian Spider monkeys at New Orleans, our port of embarkation. They would be used for a big scene near our tree house. Among that number, we reasoned, there would be a candidate who was at least as qualified as the one we had. How could any be worse? So ended our little monster's chances for a picture role.

We got our first sight of our selection when we loaded them on one of our planes at New Orleans. They were forty identical monkeys waiting for more room and action. Twenty-four hours later they became individuals as they tested the facilities in the big monkey gymnasium that had been built for them in the animal compound on Tobago. Some were much more shy than others, and, when a person entered their area, they traveled hand over hand on the bars and ropes as they headed for the high shelves that had been placed for their privacy. Others were bolder and hung motionless from the equipment to stare, quite unafraid. A few of the bolder ones were very young. Wes Dickenson, who would be in charge of them, said he would give special attention to the most responsive and try to choose the best one for us.

At first the one Wes selected for us seemed a welcome relief from the ornery little beast we had left behind. He quickly learned that he could be handled more comfortably if he didn't try to nip us. But as the end of our pre-production training time drew close, we found our generally amiable friend was still testing the anchor cord before he settled in his saddle. Jerky side glances toward the lush greenery around our work area showed "Chatto's" mind to be on something other than riding.

There would be at least one pivotal scene that called for him to separate from the dog, so there would be no way of anchoring him with an invisible cord. And by his "testing" he would know the moment he was not anchored and leave immediately. Something had to be done, and in a hurry.

Our compound included more than spacious quarters for our animals and birds. A road led from the front gate through the middle of the area so that all our creatures could be easily loaded on our trailers. On one side was a large training and rehearsal area, open except for an occasional coconut tree. We had a good place to work. We had a problem. We needed a solution. Somehow we needed to make Chatto feel that the hip collar was still in place during a scene, even when it wouldn't be used.

I chewed away on the problem while Dick worked Duke on some routine exercises. Chatto was in the saddle. He tested the anchor cord and was contented to go along for the ride while the big dog worked. It was when Dick finished the training session and Duke bounded around on "free-time" that I got the germ of an idea. The idea had germinated by the time

Dick and his dog had finished their break and walked over to where I'd been sitting on a log.

I took a ball of cord from my pocket and cut a piece that would reach from the saddle to the ground with about a foot to spare. Dick held the monkey while I removed the hip collar and attached the free end of the line directly to his body just above the hips. Immediately, he raised up to test the line, but there was no short cord for him to feel, and the slack in the longer cord gave no cue that he was tied. He became tense and still as I held him in the saddle with one hand and Duke's collar with the other.

"Walk down to that bend coconut tree, then call Duke and break and run when I give you the signal."

I kept a firm grip on the dog and monkey as Dick walked away. Duke rocked on his front feet as he sensed some kind of game. I nodded my head as Dick reached his mark and faced me, and with a mighty yell he streaked out through the trees.

It was on Duke's second bound that Chatto bailed out. The dog's speed tightened the line before the monkey hit the ground. After a series of cartwheels on the soft earth, Chatto used his speed and agility to keep on a favorable course. Tail high, he scampered alongside Duke. Twice he tried to change direction, only to be snubbed back into line by the powerful dog. When the run was finished, he sat on the ground beside the Dane. When Dick and Duke walked back to me, he hobbled alongside the dog with no thought of challenge.

"Let's go again," I told Dick.

As we set up for the next run, the monkey rose once to test for anchorage, then suddenly leaned forward and locked his strong little fingers on the saddle. This was his riding style as the dog bounded across the field. He was still in the saddle as they came back to the starting point.

They're off! At lower left, Chatto is on Duke, the Great Dane.

"He rides a lot like Longden," Dick said admiringly.

It was now time to try to outguess Chatto when there would be no line.

I fingered through the rubber bands in my tack box and selected one that I thought would fit snugly in place of the hip collar. It did, and was invisible from a few feet away. It could be used on camera if our idea worked. I placed Chatto back in the saddle. He locked his hands on the pommel before Dick walked away. His grip never changed on the run out and walk back.

"It looks like the snugness of the rubber band made him think he was still anchored," I said. "He didn't seem to want to jump."

"Jump?" Dick blurted. "He didn't even want to fall."

From the point of his surprise with the slack line and the follow-up with the rubber band, Chatto rode reliably and well. Once resigned to his role of a jockey, he came to enjoy it. His reliability and pleasure in his job was evident of an eternal truth: regardless of all the theories on learning, the best lessons are survival lessons. Or, if Father Aesop had watched Chatto's reliability he would have said: "Though many prattle much of how we learn, experience is still the bottom line."

Big Red

The Film's Story

From the novels by Jim Kjelgaard here is the warm and poignant story of a wealthy, but lonely man in need of a son, a backwoods orphan in need of a father, and the great champion Irish Setter who leads both to perilous adventure in the Canadian wilds before the strong independent personalities of man and boy are reconciled.

A 14-year-old French Canadian boy, Rene Dumont (played by Gilles Payant), fills in the void left by the war death of wealthy sportsman James Haggin's (Walter Pidgeon) son, when the boy goes to work exercising the champion Irish Setter on Haggin's estate.

Rene finds a home to love and a dog to cherish.

When Haggin separates boy and dog, so that Red can be shown at the Montreal Dog Show without Rene in the ring, the

Trainer Bill Koehler rehearses Red and Gilles for the scene shown below.

Red tries to stop the boy he loves from leaving.

dog rebels and hurls himself through a window trying to get to the boy. Before Haggin and Emile, his dog trainer, can put Red out of his misery with a hypodermic, Rene carries off Red's shattered body to his shack deep in the woods.

Rene nurses Red back to health, then reluctantly returns the dog to Haggin. False pride on the parts of Haggin and Rene prevents their reunion, and Haggin, hurt by the boy's rejection, ships Red and his mate, Mollie, to Montreal to be sold.

An obstinate female moose blocks the train long enough for Red and Mollie to escape into the rugged pine country. Haggin tells Rene of Red's and Mollie's apparently hopeless dilemma, but the boy sets out to find the dogs.

Showdog Red is unable to hunt game for his mate, who is heavy with pups. Mollie beds down in a cave, while Red forages fruitlessly for food. Then Red picks up the scent of Rene. He finds the boy and leads him to his mate.

A mountain lion, meanwhile, has stalked Mollie. Rene appears on the scene just in time to scare away the big cat.

Haggin, worried about the boy, sets off on horseback to find him. His horse rears when he gets the scent of the lion. Haggin is thrown into a gorge, and pinioned in the rocks.

Red, leading Mollie, her litter of pups and Rene back home, finds Haggin in distress. The dog stands by Haggin's side ready to fight the cat.

Just as the mountain lion springs from his rocky precipice to kill Red, Rene appears, raises his rifle, and fells the mountain lion in mid air. He frees Haggin, and man, boy and dogs head for home. Haggin tells the boy he will be working for him, living at the house, and going to school. Rene accepts gratefully.

Red holds off the mountain lion.

The Training

In casting the difficult dog part, Disney knew from long experience the importance of using the right trainer. Again, it proved to be Bill Koehler who had worked with Walt on many of his greatest pictures.

Koehler had four months to find and train an Irish Setter that could do everything but talk. Big Red had to have exceptional endurance, a stable temperament, a wide range of attitudes ranging from bounding joy to utter dejection, and above all, a firm foundation of obedience training.

After screening twenty prize Irish Setters, Koehler chose Champion Red Aye Scraps, U.D. (Utility Dog, the utmost in obedience). Scraps went through his paces with all the grace and elegance of a great champion. His skill and beauty combined in a matchless impression on the motion picture screen.

From the many marvelous feats Big Red performs in the picture, Bill Koehler reports in this book on four of the training sequences which confirmed Scraps' incredible talents and the faith Walt Disney and Bill had in the dog. The spectacular scenes Bill recalls cover the dog's tragic jump through the glass window, his feigning unconsciousness from his critical wounds, his weakness and slow recovery under Rene's care, and his wobbly gait—induced by Bill's clever "invention" and the dog's flawless cooperation—when the dog takes his first steps after the accident.

Red Crashes Through a Window

WALT DISNEY had a keen interest in the animals he starred in his pictures, but he seemed to have the warmest relationship with Big Red. This is easy to understand. Ch. Red Aye Scraps, C.D.X. was a king among dogs. He had a charisma that resulted from a combination of wholesomeness of character, intelligence and physical appeal. He was a versatile actor cast in a role that demanded all his talents. The picture showed many examples of Red's ability to change emotions in the middle of a moment. One of these was the scene where Red, locked away from the boy he had come to love, dashed wildly through the house, crashed through a window and landed in a crumpled heap on the ground.

Red was an excellent jumper, so the only problem would be to teach him, a gentleman, that it was permissible to destroy a window.

The "house-set" had been constructed on one of the stages, and it took only a few minutes for a carpenter to remove the glass, sash and all, from the window we would use, and to install a ramp that inclined from the floor to the sill.

I placed Red on a stay inside the house and crawled through the window while he watched. Because it was now only a "door," although raised and strange in appearance, Red bounded through enthusiastically when I called. I jumped him

Trainer Bill Koehler and actor Gilles Payant
are proud of their friend Big Red.

through a few more times, and decided he was ready for the next level.

One of the crew hung a clear vinyl sheet over the window opening and tacked it only at the two upper corners. I took a tuck in the lower part of the sheet and pinned it at a level that would allow Red to see a clean opening and encourage him to brush any contacting sheet out of the way. He came through a bit slowly the first time the vinyl brushed his back, but from then on ignored its touch. I pulled the pins out and let the sheet hang down to the sill. Now Red would have to make his own opening by pushing the vinyl out of the way with his head. The first time he faced the full covering he hesitated for a moment, then when it gave to his touch, he shoved on through. Within a few minutes he lunged up the ramp and plowed the vinyl aside as though it were empty space.

We removed the ramp so Red would be making a true jump from the floor through the window. For further practice and for the actual scene, I wanted him airborne, without any possibility of hesitating or aborting as might be the case with the ramp.

Now each time Red came sailing through the window to where I stood, I began to give him a "down" and "on your side" just as he touched the ground.

After another practice period on the following day, it seemed that the action and change of attitude in mid-air were close to perfect. There would be one more practice run with the vinyl just after lunch. Then the crew would quickly install a solid pane of breakaway glass, as used when an actor's face or body must go through a window. There would be absolutely no danger of a cut from such glass.

While there would be no danger of injury from the jump, there were two other difficulties that might occur. If the glass appeared greatly different than the clear vinyl, and Red became confused, there would be another period of rebuilding his confidence. And if the feel of the glass and the crash affected him, he might miss the cue to drop and go on his side.

The camera crew had set up for the shot during the lunch break. I jumped Red through the vinyl for the last time, and took him off the set while the sheet was replaced with the breakaway glass. I placed Red on a stay, went around the set and showed myself at the window until I was sure he had focused on me. I heard the word "speed" from both cameras, backed off to my working spot and called.

There was a sound of nails digging into the floor, then an instant's silence that told Red was airborne. The Red form appeared at the window and glass sprayed in all directions. I gave a command and a signal and Big Red crumpled to the floor.

There was the time of anxiety while the director checked with the camera operators.

"O.K.?" was the question.

"O.K." was the answer.

Big Red had finished the wild scene with the nearly tragic ending. Now there would be full value to the many poignant scenes that would follow.

A Rare Kind of Dog Temperament

One of the most stimulating aspects of working with an animal on a big picture is the opportunity to discover and use any unusual qualities of temperament he might possess. This is especially true in the case of a dog. A dog's peculiar action or reaction can be used to provide a required attitude.

One of Big Red's unusual qualities was an ability to relax to a state of complete inertia in almost any position. This phenomenon puzzled even Larry and Eleanor Heist who bred Red and gave him his basic obedience training. Larry found that if he picked Red up and placed him on his side, without so much as a "stay," Red would lie as though anesthetized. In the film library at Walt Disney Productions is a startling example of this quality.

There was a scene where Red, critically wounded and unconscious from the tragic jump through the window, was lying on the examination table as Walter Pidgeon and Emile Genest prepared to put him to sleep. In several takes during which Gilles Payant pleads strenuously for Red's life, and shakes the table, Red was supposed to show no sign of consciousness. Even during the Director's instructions between takes, the beautiful red dog continued to lie still. Finally, there was a take that all of us sensed was "the one." The action stopped but the camera continued to roll. We waited for the word "cut." Then with the camera still rolling, Norman Tokar, our Director, raised Red to a sitting position and gave him a pat, which Red acknowledged with animation.

There would be plenty of room on the film for the editor to remove the Director's act from the scene, but the film end would always be available to convince any skeptic that the form on the table was Red, live and alert, and not a stuffed or anesthetized dog.

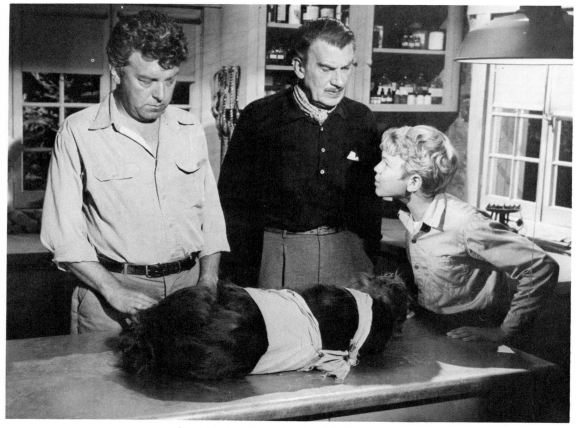

A heartbroken boy pleads with the two men
not to put the sorely wounded Red to sleep.

Red's Perfect Performance

AN IMPORTANT PROGRESSION in *Big Red* was Red's survival and recovery from the time he crashed through the window until Gilles nursed him back to health.

To portray one stage of his response to the boy's care, it was required that Red lie flat on his side and raise his head slightly to lap the oatmeal Gilles offered him with a spoon. There could be no strong gulping or other show of strength. The bedbox which had been constructed in the "cabin set" had sides about a foot high. I placed Red on his side on the bedding and positioned his head so that the Director felt he would be in the best relationship to the boy and the camera when Gilles reached out with the spoon. The carefully staged shot would look good if only Red would oblige with "weakness."

There was a final split-inch adjustment of position, with a check on the lighting.

"No rehearsal. We'll shoot it," the Director said.

Red stretched to meet the spoon on cue. He lapped at the oatmeal and swallowed weakly, hardly raising his head. It was a good take, but the Director felt there could be better coordination between Gilles' lines and the action.

On the next soft "Action," Gilles began to talk and moved the spoon toward the dog. It seemed we could feel the weakness as Red moved to lap at the food.

"Let's go again," the Director said.

This time Red took Gilles' lines and the extended spoon as his cue, with no word from me.

There is no team closeness surpassing that of a picture company which has inched its way toward the utmost value of a scene. By now each of our group was watching intently from his own position. Each one knew what was taking place. Big Red was truly feeling his part. His ability to relax in the unusual position had made it possible for him to feel the mood as well as the action. We eased into another take that seemed perfect.

"Print it and hold the others," the Director said.

The scene would convince all who saw it that our very weak dog was on his way back to health.

Big Red accepted my invitation and rose from his sickbed and stretched mightily a couple of times. He trotted buoyantly through the admiring crew to join me for a bit of well-earned exercise in a nearby grassy area.

Weak but courageous, Big Red laps oatmeal from a spoon.

How Red was "Rigged"
for a Weak, Wobbly Gait

WE KNEW that one of the most important sequences in Red's recovery could be his first successful effort to walk, providing that his wobbly gait appeared natural. I have long believed that a limp or other disability that is "taught" is so rhythmic that it is obviously an act. There is a better way to get the attitude and action, but only if a dog will accept without resistance a sensation that is strange but not at all painful. It was that kind of an acceptance I hoped for as I prepared Red for the scene where he was to stagger weakly into camera and toward the bed where Gilles was watching.

I linked some light, very strong rubber bands together and ran them across Red's body behind his shoulders, crossed them under his chest, then tied an end to each front leg above its pastern. I rigged another chain of bands across his loin and attached the ends above his hocks. I ran a third string under his body from his right elbow to his left stifle to hamper his extension a bit. It would be easy to hide the rubbers with his hair, but now I was interested only in how effectively I had rigged him. I brought him toward me on a slow walk. It looked good. The elasticity of the rubber bands caused whichever foot was raised to come up fast which caused his weight to lurch to the opposite side. The diagonal rubbers caused a further unsteadiness to his gait.

Red was not uncomfortable. He was totally unconcerned. But there could be no more practice before we shot the scene, lest the dog adjust to the tension and lose the unsteadiness. As I removed the rigging, I hoped there would be no camera trouble or other complications which could make us go for more than one take and give Red that chance to "adjust."

Two days later the set-up was made for the scene, and with it came a problem that seemed to be without solution. Big Red would have to walk into the room and toward the bed. I would have to be in front of him to focus and slow him. But it seemed there was no way the camera position could give me a reasonable place to work. Red and the boy on the bed would both be on camera throughout the whole shot. There was that silence on the stage that means everyone is trying to find a way through the same stone wall.

The silence was broken when the operator suggested that if the camera were raised a bit more it might not reach much of the area under the bed, making it possible for me to lie on my side between the floor and bedspring. Another observed that the bed was so low that the space would not accommodate an adult. But it was our one chance without a major revision of the set-up; so the crew went to work.

Quickly, Set Decorating brought in some risers that attached to the legs and raised the bed several inches. An electrician focused a small light on the area where I would lie so Red would be able to see me. There would be no room to use a signal but at least I could give Red a visible target as I tried to talk him slowly to Gilles who would sit on the bed.

I put the rigging on Red and left him standing just off-camera. The camera was up to speed when I worked my way backwards under the bed, and gave Red a prayerful "Easy." He came wobbling into the shot on unsteady legs, looking too weak to take the next step. Because I was directly beneath Gilles, Red's focus on me was in the right direction. He wobbled closer, and I could see only his legs beneath the level of the bedspring. I knew that I was lost to his sight, and hoped he would not try to crouch down to see me, but continue the last few feet to the boy he had been sent to so many times. I held my breath as he drew so close that I knew his head must be at the boy's knees. I tried to visualize him being responsive to Gilles, and not wondering where I was.

The sounds from the set let me know that the shot I had not seen was a good one. I let my breath out slowly and relaxed for a few moments as I stared up at the bedspring and said something that I would repeat many times on the picture.

"What a dog!"

Red takes a few tottering steps on the road to recovery.

Bodger, Tao and Luath—the tired and homesick trio.

The Incredible Journey

The Film's Story

Adapted from the international best-selling novel of the same name by Sheila Burnford, this Disney masterpiece is a live-action, warm, exciting adventure story of three animals, a Bull Terrier, a Labrador Retriever and a Siamese cat that travel 250 miles across the Canadian wilderness to return to their home.

Professor Jim Hunter (John Drainie), his wife (Sandra Scott), and their two children Peter, (Ronald Cohoon) and Elizabeth (Marion Finlayson), depart their little Canadian university town for England where the professor has a summer teaching assignment. They leave their two dogs and cat in the temporary care of a family friend, writer John Longridge

(Emile Genest), who lives some 250 miles away in the north-western part of the great sprawling province of Ontario.

Bodger, the Bull Terrier, belongs to 11-year-old Peter; the golden Labrador Retriever, named Luath, is Jim Hunter's favorite hunting companion, and Tao, the Siamese cat, is the beloved pet of 9-year-old Elizabeth.

The three animals become restive and lonesome for home. When Longridge leaves on a hunting trip and does not take them with him, the animals believe that they are unwanted and set out across the unknown terrain to get back to the Hunter home.

The domesticated pets face the unknown wilds with its denizens, human and animal. They encounter a number of dangerous and wonderful adventures. Tao, a great hunter, out-maneuvers a stalking lynx. Bodger meets and beats a vicious farm dog, saving Luath from death. Together, the three fight off an attacking bear.

Wild animals are not the only problems confronting a little party on the trail; survival is the all-important factor. Bodger is a fighter but no hunter, and Luath, an expert at retrieving, has nothing to retrieve. It is Tao who has the brains of the threesome and generally quarterbacks the venture.

Wherever they go the trio seems to leave some good behind them. They befriend a gentle old hermit. Tao is loved by a lonely little Finnish girl who rescues the Siamese from drowning and nurses it back to health.

Luath, after an encounter with a porcupine, is found wounded by a farmer. He brings the dog home to his wife and together they remove the quills and care for him. The couple enjoy his company for a short while, but the pull to return home is greater than their hold on the animal. He rejoins his friends, and the trek continues.

Meanwhile, the three have now been given up for lost. No one believes that they can survive the rugged terrain. The Hunters return to a saddened home, only to be overjoyed at the unexpected appearance of a trio of straggly-looking but healthy four-footers. Bodger, Luath and Tao have successfully completed their incredible journey.

The Training

The Incredible Journey reflects Walt Disney's own incredible genius for converting a great novel from print to a magnificent motion picture. This film also confirms the amazing talents of Bill Koehler and his associate trainers in working with animals — often against their natural instincts — to perform seemingly impossible actions to perfection.

How do you get a disinterested Bull Terrier and a dog-hating cat to develop a warm and real affection for each other? How do you get a cat to cross a stream "on the rocks?" — or to roll in an exact spot on the ground without the help of a human hand? And a mother bear and her cubs to interact with the dogs and cat according to the script!!! What do you do for a scene that calls for the animals to cross a snow-covered log when the snow melts? In the following chapters Bill Koehler discloses the ingenious methods he and his friends used to obtain the desired "takes," and how a fine veterinarian, Dr. Cormack, quickly cured their sick cats without a delay in the film's production schedule.

"Warm and Real" Affection
Between Dog and Cat

THERE ARE many attitudes and actions that can be made part of an animal's behavior by training and conditioning. But true, demonstrative friendship is not one of them.

Early in our pre-production talks, James Algar, Executive Producer of *The Incredible Journey,* emphasized that one of the most important qualities of our picture would be a warm and real affection between Bodger, the Bull Terrier and Tao, the Siamese cat.

"Warm and real" were uppermost in my mind when I introduced Bodger and Tao. Good obedience training had brought Bodger to where he regarded distractions as cues to be mindful of his own conduct. He was indifferent to the cat. The cat, however, sent crescending yowls from the safety of a wire cage while I worked Bodger in some basic exercises nearby. These included a Down-Stay about two feet from the cage. The Stay brought Tao's yowls to the top of the scale. I heaped praise on Bodger for ignoring all the insults.

A few days of such work showed that Bodger's indifference had reassured the cat and that tolerance had replaced the earlier suspicions. But it can be a long way from tolerance to "warm and real" friendship. We trusted that the "marching order" in our story could do much to show the character and relationship of our animals. Luath, the young Labrador Retriever, would lead the way as they trekked through the wilderness.

About ten feet behind him and five feet off to his right would be Bodger, "the old dog." Tao, the cat, was a free spirit and would follow his own whims to all parts of the traveling scenes, but remain concerned with the movement of the dogs, and receptive to a bell signal.

Hal and I set up a program that would teach each dog, separately, a slow, tired walk and stop, and the cat to come from a box on signal and join the dogs. We would put it all together in "the marching order" as soon as all three animals were qualified. Bodger had a solid recall and progressed a bit faster than Luath, who had to be given basic training along with his picture work. But within two weeks Hal and I decided to see how well we could hold the two in position. The dogs had spent lots of leisure time together and were not distracted by each other. We worked hard for several periods a day training the dogs to hold a standing position while we went to positions as far as two hundred feet from them. We practiced moving them in the tired attitude of the trek. Sometimes I would stop Bodger and hold him while Luath would look back at him with concern. Their performance took on a perfect naturalness.

About this time Al Niemela came to my kennel to complete Tao's training and to give us the third handler we would need on the picture. Because of Al's good work and the cat's tolerance for the dogs, we decided to take the crucial step. We would try the "full marching order"—all three animals working in unison while we hoped for the best in action and in that much more elusive quality: attitude.

We mocked up a "set" in a big field and left the two dogs standing in their starting positions. Al placed his trip box about twenty feet behind the Bull Terrier, then stretched out his trip cord and joined us at what we had set for our "camera position."

Hal and I started the dogs in their slow, exhausted walk. Al jerked his cord and the door flew open. Tao froze for a moment, then came after the dogs at a fast trot. He held his tail straight up. A vibrato yowl, keyed to the rhythm of his trot, expressed his indignation at being left behind. He interrupted the yowl long enough to spit as he passed close to the Bull Terrier.

Bodger disregarded the insult and wagged his tail cordially without changing his gait. Our hopes raised, then dropped, as Tao went on by without response. He was close behind Luath when our practice pattern ended.

"Pretty good for the first time," Hal said cheerfully. "Good control."

But any of us would have traded some of the control for a pinch of "warm and real affection."

Two months later we were still waiting for Tao to thaw out and respond to Bodger's friendly attitude with something other than hisses and an upraised paw. Now, as we looked at the road that was to be the setting for the first shot of our picture, we were confident that we could control our moving pattern at any distance. We were not so confident on getting the attitude that would put the meaning into our beautiful mechanics.

The road's wheel tracks were two paths that showed hints of the brown earth through the cover of grass and small blue flowers. Moss-covered rail fences held the road to one narrow lane. A stump pasture sloped away from one side of the road, and second growth timber formed a dark wall on the other. Beyond where the road sank behind a low rise, firs and cedars stood against churning clouds. We spaced our animals while Jack Couffer and Lloyd Beebe set up their cameras. There would be a change. Tao would come from the trip box, under the rail and onto the road from the righthand side. As a free spirit, he could join the march at will. I hoped that his position would make him appear at least interested in the "old and tired" Bodger.

"After he's on the road, do you think you can get him to jump up on the fence and walk along the rails?" Jack asked.

Al studied the geography of the shot for a moment. "Let's give it a try."

We took our working positions near the cameras, which were set in the middle of the road to face the dogs from over a hundred feet away. The switches clicked. "We've got speed," Jack said. "Bring 'em on."

As we had done so many times in training, Hal and I started Luath and Bodger on their tired walk. There was a far away click of the trip box. After seconds that seemed like minutes, a small figure entered the right sideline and headed for the middle of the road. At a fast trot that jarred his protesting yowl into a vibrato, he closed the gap that had opened wider than we had intended. Without a show of interest, he passed Bodger and drew close behind Luath.

"Jump," Al called, and swung his arm to the right. Tao angled sharply toward the fence and jumped to the mossy top rail, where, tail high, he resumed his trot.

"Stop 'em. Let the cat catch up," Jack said.

The interval between the two dogs held as they stopped the tired walk. Then, as Tao's profanity drew nearer, their heads turned to face him. Tao dropped lightly down from the rail and came out to where the old dog stood watching. Then, from cheek to tail, he began to rub against Bodger's front legs. He leaned so hard that the dog's look of surprise softened as he recognized the cat's honest affection.

Tao's rubbing settled into a rhythm. Slowly, the dog's nose came down to touch the cat's head. Emotion drew his ears even closer together as the cat's rubbing included his muzzle.

Luath watched the activity and wagged his tail approvingly as Tao threaded his way between and around the terrier's front legs.

"Bring 'em out," Jack said.

Tao was still trying to rub as we signalled the dogs for a continuation of the journey.

"Cut," Jack called. "We've got it! What a nice way to start a picture."

He had it. No one who would see *The Incredible Journey* could doubt the affection between Bodger and Tao. It was "warm and real."

Stream-Crossing Siamese

IT SEEMED to be a much better place for a picnic than a project. The shiny little stream slid through the new green of the pasture and spilled over the rocky places in millions of sequins. In places it narrowed to straight channels that moved between the low banks with quiet dignity. It was at one of the wider places that our director stopped and pointed.

"This should do. It's too wide for the cat to jump, and it'll give enough room for the music," Jack said. He grinned as the four of us continued to stand in the warm spring sun on a day that was made more for absorbing than working. "Let's get a few of those big ones," he prompted. "And don't mess up the set."

From bars of black sand up and down the stream we wrenched big stones that would be large enough to protrude from the water when placed where we had chosen. To "save the set," we carried our selection through the water to their places. Carefully, we tipped and rolled each stone around on the small rocks and gravel of the bottom until all sat solidly with their tops a few inches above the shining waters in a variety of forms and colors. Finally, they formed stepping stones that extended from within two feet of one bank to within four feet of the other.

"They're too much in line," Jack said. "If the cat has to zig and zag a bit, the action will be better from both cameras. And the composers will have more to work with when they score music to his moves."

Because of the positive characters of our three animals in *The Incredible Journey,* we took every opportunity to show their interaction with a wilderness environment. The use of stones by Tao to cross a stream could be a part of our traveling sequence. The writer's idea of scoring music to the cat's moves was a natural—if the moves were right. We tilted and rolled some more.

"What do you think, Al?" Jack asked our cat trainer.

Al studied the stones. "One or two will be turning him a bit too much from our target spot."

There was some more tilting and rolling.

"Now how does it look?" Jack asked.

Al nodded. "Let's try it."

Jack and Lloyd jockeyed around for camera positions while Al brought his choice of cats from the van. "I'll go with 'Notch.' He'll work around water."

Before he began a career as Syn's "double," "Notch" had been a street brawler of great prowess. Another tomcat with a suicidal complex had lasted long enough to split the tip of an ear and give "Notch" his call name.

The rest of our six man crew sprawled on the warm grass as Al rehearsed his cat from the trip box which he had placed on one side of the creek to the first stone of our "crossing."

Al loves all kinds of animals and tells them so in various ways, including pep talks. "Atta boy, Notch. Notch knows it's dry on the stones. Let's try it once more."

Again, Notch came from the box to the edge of the stream and jumped to the first stone where he had "discovered" a tidbit near the bell and had received Al's enthusiastic approval.

"He's heading right. Now I'll rehearse him all the way across."

"We'll shoot the rehearsal," Jack said.

Al put Notch back in the trip box and checked to see that there was no slack in the cord that ran to the hand of one of our crew who sat on the bank twenty feet downstream. Al waded across the creek and crouched, aligned with the route of the stones, safely out of frame for both cameras.

While we waited for the sand that had churned up from Al's steps to clear, we enjoyed the beauty of our little set. The shining water, our carefully placed stones and the background of the green field were idyllic. Cooperative meadowlarks strutted and fluttered in the right locations.

"Let's try it," Jack said.

Al's bell began to ring, then he nodded. The trip-door opened. Notch came out and purposefully entered the scene on his way to the first stone. He landed, head extended intently toward the second stone. Sinewy cat, shining water, green field—it was a beautiful scene. Then Notch jumped into the water and swam across the creek and walked to where Al stood, his bell silenced.

"Like I said," Al reminded us, "Notch doesn't mind the water."

Between the towels in my van and the warm sun, Notch was soon readied for another try. Al rehearsed him in a progressive pattern from the last stone to the bell, then, backing off a stone at a time, until he was starting from the trip box.

"Now he knows the route," Al assured us.

There was a final check all around. It seemed everything was in the cat's favor and ours. Al's bell rang. The door flew open. Notch jumped to the first stone. He measured the distance to the second stone. Disdaining the easy distance, he jumped into the water and swam across. His wet and sinewy body mirrored the sun as he came from the water, and with an obnoxious Siamese dignity, walked up to where Al was staring at him.

"He just doesn't mind the water," Al said. "I'll try Tao."

Notch was toweled and left exposed to the sun's warmth, while Al rehearsed Tao. The rest of us dissolved our identities and became part of the spring day.

Finally, Al brought us back to the reality of production. "He's ready."

The bell rang. The door opened. Tao entered the scene on his way to the first stone. Then, as though projected by something other than his own efforts, Tao bounced in high arcs from one stone to another with a tempo that would inspire delight in any composer. We waited for the word from the two cameras. Both had gotten all of it.

"Great. We've had a good morning," Jack said. "Let's eat."

As was our custom, we looked around at the set before leaving.

"Our stones look natural," Jack said. "We'll leave them there."

Hal Driscoll, my partner, was still sprawled on the warm earth. He rolled onto his side and looked at the big stones we had rolled. "Yeah, let's leave them there. Somebody else's cat might want to get across."

Cool Cat and Hot Sand

JACK COUFFER pointed at a bare spot in the middle of the road. "It will really be in character if we can get Tao to stop and roll on that spot, and then run to catch up with the dogs. How can we get him to roll without any training?"

I had no quick answer. Often in an animal picture a director will see an opportunity for an action that was not included in pre-production training, but which could add much to a sequence. Then a trainer must bet on his knowledge of sensory appeals. It generally adds up to a one-shot chance without a trial or rehearsal. I could think of only one possibility:

"We can try to make him feel like rolling. We'll need a fire and something to heat some sand in."

Del, one of our crew, left in his pickup to find a container, and the rest of us snapped branches from fallen fir, and soon had a fire crackling about twenty feet from the trail. The chill in the air made the fire a comfort as we waited for Del to return. Some of the flames had flattened into coals as the pickup came lurching up the grade between the trees and stumps. Del had brought a trough that had been made by cutting an oil drum lengthwise. We nestled it onto the coals and filled it half full of the sandy soil.

While the sand heated, we made an approach shot of our cat emerging from the timber.

The air still held its chill when we gave the sand a last stir and spread it on the bare spot as Jack directed. He used a fir bough to sweep it into a strip slightly wider than the path and about six feet long.

We hurried to position our cast for the shot; the Labrador in front, the Bull Terrier ten feet back and to the Lab's right. The cat's trip box was about twenty feet behind Bodger, well concealed by a low cedar limb. We moved down and stood as close to the camera as possible.

Within the next few seconds, I sorted through all of the "ifs" that were involved in the shot. If our calculations were right the dogs would clear camera just at the time the cat reached the warm sand. If the sand had the feel of sun-warmed ground and the air was chilly enough, sensory appeal would make the cat want to roll.

I heard the camera whir and Jack say, "Bring 'em on."

Hal and I brought the dogs toward us at their pained, exhausted walk. Luath, then Bodger, reached and crossed the sand without any reaction to the temperature, and I wondered if their concentration was completely the result of training, or if the sand had cooled rapidly.

"Cat," Jack said.

Al tripped the cat box, and all of us watched the cat burst from beneath the cedar limb. Tao stopped and stared at the dogs as they neared the camera. Then he broke into a high-tailed trot, so rough that the protests seemed to be jarred from him, rather than emitted. He crossed the warm sand without a reaction. Then, as he feet reached cold ground, the contrast registered. He turned back onto the warm area. He crouched with the side of his head on the warmth. With joyous abandon he tumbled onto his side and rolled—and rolled—and rolled.

"That's enough," Jack said. "Call him out, Al."

Syn flipped to his feet when he heard Al's bell. With both tail and voice high with appreciation, he came out of camera.

Jack smiled in his tongue-in-cheek way. "Gee, that was easy, wasn't it?"

I didn't think about answering him. I thought about how relaxing it might be to walk out and roll on the hot sand.

It's one more river to cross for the three travelers.

A Slick Scene

THE LOG was beautiful. Some of its roots extended vertically and others were still buried in the driftwood and debris of the small island where it had grown as a mighty fir. It ran about fifteen feet above the rocky stream bed and across a deep pool to rest on the far bank where the pool was turned sharply by the face of a mountain. The bark on its topside had been worn away by years of rain and snow and creatures that used it. Now it was a path covered lightly with snow.

"Place them to cross in the usual order," Jack Couffer said. "And don't worry about your own tracks. They won't show from our angle."

Hal looked down at the rocks and cold water. "Oh, then I guess there's nothing to worry about," he said as he joined me in favoring bare wool socks over slippery boot soles.

Hal and I used the roots for a ladder to climb onto the log. We took our dogs as they were handed up to us and placed them in position. We studied the log while Al nestled Syn's trip box among the roots in a position that would send the cat after the dogs. The narrow path would pose no challenge to the traction and low center of gravity of our animals, but Hal and I could not straddle the log and worm our way across, lest we disturb the snow on its sides; so we left our dogs on a stay and began to inch our way across.

Luath leads the way across the icy water.

Brave Bodger crosses the slippery log.

Tao takes his turn.

The rocks and water seemed to get farther away and the log narrower as we progressed. Earth finally appeared beneath the end of the log and we dropped off to face our dogs with our heads almost at their level. The crossing was easy for the dogs and a romp for the cat.

Jack looked over at us from his camera position and grinned at our obvious appreciation for the dry, wide earth.

"We'll settle for that one," he said. "We'll send the film in today, and we'll soon know how they like it."

Four days later an enthusiastic report came from the studio.

"They like it," Jack said as he hung up the phone.

I looked at my partner's relieved face. "They like it, Hal. Now we won't have to go back," I told him.

"Oh yes we will," Jack told us. "They like the sequence so well they want individual shots of each animal, and another angle from a higher point." Jack waited while Hal and I observed a few moments of silence. "Let's load up."

On our way out of town to the log, we stopped our van behind Lloyd Beebe's station wagon at a market and waited until Jack came out with two large sacks and a big grin.

"Why's he grinning?" Hal asked.

I had no answer as we moved on toward our location. A half hour later we were again staring at the log.

"It's no longer than it was," Jack said cheerfully.

"Hey, look!" Hal said. "The snow's melted." He pointed at the slippery log. "You can't shoot the top of the log without snow. It won't match. We might as well move to something else."

"We can make it match," Jack said. He went to the nearby station wagon and took some boxes from the mysterious sacks.

"Oh, no!" Hal groaned. "Snowflakes!"

We watched him hand a few boxes to the sure-footed Lloyd.

"You've got no worry," Jack assured us. "They're absolutely pure and we won't pollute the stream."

"They won't, but we might," Hal answered.

Lloyd quickly finished the decorating job, and once more we placed our animals and began our trip across the log. Hal, in the lead, had passed over the pool and saw the comfort of dry land a few feet below. He began to laugh.

"Jack forgot to tell us the melting snow brought the creek up and it's not quite so far down to the water. Look down!"

"I don't want to," I whispered out of the middle of my mouth. "Quit laughing—you're shaking the log!"

With Six Animals,
You Need Luck

MAKING PICTURES is hard at best. When it is necessary to time the pivotal actions of several characters in a scene, the job can be doubly hard.

Our cast of three principals in *The Incredible Journey* had been well prepared to work together, but now there would be the complication of three more characters that were strange to us and strange, very strange, to our dogs and cat. One was a large black bear. The other two were cubs of the same variety.

Carol, the adult, was owned by John Welty who had demonstrated to us that the big bear was reliable when working at liberty around distractions which included other animals. But the cubs, borrowed for the scene, were another matter. Comparatively, bears are among the smaller creatures at birth, but they're born with full blown appetites. They can be depended upon to head for where they believe there is food, or go back to where they had found it. They also have a very rough way of checking out the edibility of any strange object. The cubs were the unpredictable factor in our thinking as we stood by the set and considered all the actions that would go into our master shot.

The old Bull Terrier was to lie exhausted and starving at the bottom of a grassy knoll, with his friend Tao on guard a few feet behind him. The cubs, according to the script, were to come tumbling into the scene, and "discover" the Bull Terrier. Regardless of any examination by the cubs, Bodger would be required to remain "exhausted and unable to move." Enter, then, the big bear from behind the knoll, reared on hind legs to her full eight feet to menace the dog who dared to be so close to her cubs. At this point Tao, swollen to twice his normal size by fury, would challenge the mother who would pause in the face of the threat. Then, Luath was to return from a hunt bearing food for Bodger; quickly evaluate the situation and join in the defense of his friend. The bear, impressed by the combined forces, was to pirouette away from the threat and, trusting her cubs to follow, drop down on all fours and leave the set.

We checked off the probabilities and questionable areas.

Bodger had the most difficult role. He was solid on "stays" and would not see danger in the actions of the bears and, hopefully, would hold even when examined by the cubs. Tao, if not introduced, would oppose anything from a gopher to the National Guard, and would show the right attitude toward the bear. Luath would come onto the set when called, and react to the bear. To condition the cubs, we decided to give them a lot of concentrated experience in entering the set and finding food close to prominent objects. That left the big bear and a problem. John Welty could call Carol onto the set and make her rear up by being in front of her and a short distance off camera. But John could not be in two places at once. He would have to be in front of the set to get Carol to rear up and enter the set. But to get her turn, drop to all fours, and leave the scene, he would have to be behind the set to time the turn and call out.

"I'll have to be on Carol heavy to keep her on her hind

legs, and nobody could turn her away from me," John explained. "Otherwise Connie could call her out."

Connie, John's daughter, was second to John in the bear's affection, but not even she could cut into Carol's concentration on her father.

As was often the case, it was my partner, Hal Driscoll, who came up with an off-beat idea.

"Suppose we could make her turn away from you at just the right time—could Connie get her to come out then?"

"Probably," John answered. "But how can you turn her?"

"With a light piece of black cable," Hal said. "It won't show in the picture. If I can give her a little tug backwards when she is standing straight up, she'll turn in the direction I tip her."

"It would have to be perfect," John told him. "If she is leaning forward when you tug, she'll ignore it."

"Then it'll be perfect," said Hal the optimist.

We needed Hal's optimism a few days later when we prepared to shoot the big scene. The Bull Terrier and the cat were in their places on the set and the other animals were in position to be brought into the shot.

There was the sound of the cameras and a squeak as a crate was opened. We optimists stared at the right side of the knoll from where, the script said, "The cubs would come wrestling and tumbling into the set, locked tightly together until they would break apart." Like projectiles they came, they wrestled, they tumbled and then broke apart. They realized they were in the area where they had often found food. Their appetites drove them frantically around the set. They saw Bodger, and stopped prospecting. They came over and sniffed at the strange white creature. They nuzzled and nibbled with no response from a dog that appeared too exhausted to move.

"Call Carol," the Director said.

Bear cub plays with Bodger.

Facing the angry mother bear.

Johnny called, and, as soon as the bear came over the knoll, cued her to rear up and move toward the dog and cubs.

As the monster came closer, the cat inflated and yowled.

"Call Luath," Jack said.

Luath charged into camera toward the big bear.

John had Carol at the highest part of her rear, with one powerful paw raised threateningly above her head. Then, confronted by the cat and Labrador, she rocked back a step, pivoted sharply away and dropped to all fours, her body and attention turned away from John. She ambled swiftly from sight toward Connie's call.

Hal's tension on the cable had been exquisite. "There's only one thing wrong," he said as he came from the rear of the set to join us. "When the writer sees this scene, he's gonna think he's perfectly rational."

Maude rides the hermit's head but keeps an eye on the cat that follows.

Syn and the Other
Siamese Become Ill

BARNEY, our crow, might have been the first of his kind to fly at five hundred miles an hour. He had flown from Vancouver to Toronto along with my son Dick, Al Niemela and me. In nine other crates were three Bull Terriers, two Labradors and four Siamese cats.

We had finished our work on the wilderness scenes for *The Incredible Journey,* and James Algar, Walt Disney's Associate Producer on that picture, had arranged for us to arrive in Toronto three weeks before production would resume. This would give us time to establish our animals comfortably in their new quarters and to familiarize them with the environment of the sound stages and the few exterior locations we would use. Adequate pre-production work with animals is most important to their happiness and performance. Preparation for any picture is against "the day of reckoning" when production starts and lack of readiness can be costly. Adequate pre-production time has long been one reason why the Disney animals do a good job.

"Let's load up and go check out the 'hermitage set,' " I told Al and Dick the morning after we landed in Toronto.

We drove about twenty-five miles through the fragrant summer countryside until we reached the bridge that was our landmark, and turned into a rutted lane. Our first view told us the hermitage was "for real." It was the actual residence of a friendly old gentleman. The picturesque cabin, the low animal shelters, with walls and roofs so insulated with straw that they resembled igloos, were enough to make any location scout cry "Eureka!"

As animal trainers, we three were concerned with more than the pictorial appeal. The hermit's livestock would provide our dogs with a tempting buffet of odors. Birds, bold and active, skirmished in the tall grass and weeds bordering the path that twisted its way up from the sparkling creek, up the steep hill and turned sharply between the cabin and shed to the hermit's front door.

We walked slowly and studied the path from cabin to creek and back again. Then we took our first team from the van and went by a roundabout way to the starting point at the creek.

The script called for the cat to follow close behind the hermit and menace the crow that would ride on the man's head. Next would come the old Bull Terrier, then, reluctantly, the Labrador would follow behind bearing a rabbit he had caught. We rehearsed the animals in that order until they were moving slowly along the path in response to our commands and signals. Our "resident hermit" watched from a vantage point in his barnyard. There was concern on his face as we finished work for the day and started to load the van. He pointed to the path.

"There's lots of bugs in the weeds and grass," he told us. "If I were you, I'd check those animals real good."

I thanked him for his thoughtfulness, and told him we'd be back the next day.

The trip back to the studio lot where our animals were

quartered was a pleasant drive of an hour. All of us, humans and animals alike, were relaxed from the activities of the day.

"Well," Al said, "I feel a little better about it now."

"Went good," I agreed. "But Dick's got the hard part. He'll need to work on getting Luath to split off by the shed and bury the rabbit. He can work on that separately tomorrow."

When we reached the studio, we took each dog and cat to a weathered set that was stored near our cat runs.

Open in front, it had a roof and a floor, and the counter across one side made an excellent utility table. Now it was our examination table as we checked each animal that had been exposed to the weeds at the hermitage, paying extra attention to the ears and the area between the toes before an animal was put in its run. We saw no ticks or parasites of any kind.

"The hermit was really concerned about insects," Dick said.

The shadows on the studio's back lot were long when we put the last of our animals in their runs.

The next day's work at the hermitage was even easier. We had the feel of the path and the interval between the animals was easier to hold. I checked the positions where the camera setups would be made, so I could approximate the distance and angles from where we would work. Again, our friend, the hermit, watched and grinned in appreciation of the animals' performance.

"That old man really likes animals," Al said as we finished loading for the trip back to Toronto.

The next morning as we rounded the corner of the studio, each dog was rearing and ready at his gate. Dick and I greeted them all by name and started our kennel work. Al had begun his conversation with his beloved cats which were quartered about thirty feet from our dogs. The loquacious Siamese had found a kindred soul in Al Niemela and Al's personal remarks to each of them, and their guttural replies were fun to hear. But on this morning there were no replies. Al's own silence caught my attention and I hurried over to where he stood motionless in front of the cattery.

"Something's wrong," Al said.

The cats were motionless. They were lying with their feet under them in the way of cats at rest. It was as though a taxidermist had mounted one on the shelf or floor of each pen. We began to examine them. We took temperatures and checked for discharge from eyes or noses. We double checked for external parasites. We discussed the possibility of food or water poisoning, and checked the pens and litter boxes for signs of intestinal upset. There was none. All of our cats had been immunized as completely as possible against the common cat diseases, and other evidence ruled out communicable illnesses. Quartered next to our Siamese "cast" were six cats we had rented locally to play a small part in a barnyard scene. We studied them carefully. There was no sign of sickness.

"We'll stay in and work Bodger, Luath and Barney on the stage today," I told Dick and Al. "In the meantime, I'll try to locate the most experienced veterinarian on cats in the area. It'll take a good one to figure this out."

Providence led me through a chain of phone calls from which I learned that a Dr. Cormack was highly regarded by knowledgeable cat fanciers in the Toronto vicinity. I called his office. I had a hunch that any diagnosis must include something more than an examination of the cats themselves, and was relieved to learn that Dr. Cormack would revise his schedule to give him the time he would need to come over and talk with us instead of asking that the cats be brought to his hospital.

By re-scheduling some appointments and canceling others, he would be able to come to the studio early the next afternoon. In the meantime, it was important that we continue our observations.

Dick was working with Luath and the crow when I returned to the stage. Al was standing by a table near the open stage door. Syn, our best cat and Al's favorite, was on the table in the same stuffed and mounted posture that we had observed in the pens. Al shook his head as I drew near.

"He won't do a thing. He won't even turn toward the bell. He won't even turn his head to drink water."

I tried to sound cheerful as I filled Al and Dick in on my conversation with Dr. Cormack. While we were talking, Disney producer James Algar came onto the stage to check progress on the set. A producer wrestles with a lot of detail, all against a deadline, and we did not want to bother him unnecessarily. Now with production only two weeks away, I had to give him the bad news.

I'll always be grateful for the calmness that is part of Jim Algar's character. His first thoughts and his sympathy went to the cats and their trainer, although he was responsible for the efficiency of production and its costs.

He looked to where Syn was a pathetic lump on the table. "They're all like that?"

"All four of them," Al answered.

I told Jim about our report to Dr. Cormack and the doctor's instructions to us.

"What do you think we should do?" Jim asked.

Al said, "To play it safe, we'd better phone Lloyd Beebe and tell him to stand by to ship us some of our other Siamese cats. It'll be tough, but there'll be nothing else to try if Syn isn't in shape."

Jim nodded his agreement. "Call him."

Our cats made another change in appearance by nightfall. They had a wizened look as though they were disappearing within their own skins. The luminous quality was gone from their coats. Each of the four was a distinctive character and a friend to the three of us, and we felt the numbness known to those who love a creature that is suffering a mysterious illness. We tried to give the cats a little water from a syringe. Each rejected it with a violent shake of his head.

"They don't even want to swallow," Al said.

The long night was not for sleeping, but for sorting over again all details of our sick cats' environment.

The next morning we ignored the greetings of our dogs and rushed straight from our van to the cat pens. The abstinence from food and water and the illness had caused a devastating change. A general atrophy had changed the cats' expressions. All resiliency had gone from the skin, which, when folded between a thumb and forefinger, held the shape in which it was released. Now our problem was twofold. First, to save the lives of our cats. Second, to identify their illness so we could protect other cats from the same agony.

It was early afternoon when a security man admitted Dr. Cormack to the back lot.

Everyone whose life has been intensely involved with animals has come to have a great respect for the diagnostic abilities of a top veterinarian, who must evaluate and treat without any verbal communication with his patient. Within a few minutes we knew Dr. Cormack was one of the finest. He had the confidence of a man who knows what he's doing and exactly how to do it. With the deftness and purpose that comes from great experience, he examined our cats. Then he began to ask questions.

"What about food and water?"

"A mix of dry food and meat," I told him. "The same that our nondescript cats have been getting."

"Could they have eaten anything on the stage that the others didn't get?" he asked.

"Nothing," I told him.

He kept probing. "Where else did you have the Siamese that the other cats didn't go?"

"Only out to the farm where we worked."

"Could they have picked up anything to eat there?"

"No. We were watching them all the while they were out of their carriers."

"I think we can rule out food poisoning. But it's a poison. Was there any weed spray where you were working them?"

"The weeds looked green and clean," I told him.

"They've got the symptoms that go with chemical poisoning. I'm going to give them an injection of Vitamin K. If we're on the right track, they should react favorably within a few hours." He hesitated and turned back on the way to his car. "Give me a call toward evening."

Dick and I worked most of the day with our dogs and the crow, and Al, unable to work his cats, spent his time watching them. It was about four hours after Dr. Cormack's visit that we heard Al yell.

"Syn just drank—by himself. Syn drank! They're all feeling better. My cats are feeling better."

It seemed to contradict all physiological patterns but a change had already come over the cats. As though freed from an evil spell, all four were responding to Al's grateful tones.

I went to the studio office and called Dr. Cormack.

"We're not home free yet," he said. "But it looks good. I'll be there again tomorrow afternoon. But keep checking for chemicals. Otherwise, you'll have to wash the cats after every time you work them, or they could be contaminated and lick something from their feet and bodies again. The big thing is to re-examine every place where they've been."

Early the next morning we cared for our animals, and checked the cats carefully before leaving them for another trip to the country. We wanted to be certain that they had continued to improve before we left them for the time it would take to check the hermitage thoroughly.

With backs arched and tails carried high, they strutted and responded to Al's greetings. It was especially good to hear Al and Syn carry on one of their conversations.

"Syn says he feels good and wants to ride along," Al interpreted. He hesitated a moment as he fished for another reason. "Besides, I could watch him better if he's with me."

"You surely could, Al," I agreed. "Load him and let's go."

Our resident hermit waved from the porch as we stopped near the cabin door. He listened sympathetically as we told him of our experience with the cats, and how it seemed certain that they had licked a chemical from their feet or bodies.

"Can you remember spraying around her with any residual weed spray?" I asked him.

The brow above his whiskered face wrinkled thoughtfully. "I've never sprayed for weeds around here. In fact, the only spraying I've done lately was with sheep dip."

"Where?" I asked him.

He nodded toward the path. "There—where you worked your animals. Remember me tellin' you the weeds were full of bugs? I sprayed the whole path from the creek up to the cabin. I thought it might make it better for your animals. But I guess it didn't." The kindly old man shook his head remorsefully. "I'll never do that again."

Cresylic acid! The cats had licked cresylic acid.

The smile finally came back to the old man's face, as we took turns reassuring him that the cats were on the mend, and now we knew what to guard against.

The scattered cumulus clouds had gathered together. United, they sent an opening salvo of fat drops against the dusty roof of the van and then settled into a tempo that promised to be with us for a while.

"This will take care of that sheep dip," I yelled to the hermit as I followed the others into the van.

The drive back to the studio was a happy one. The singing and splashing of the tires on the wet road and the smell of steaming macadam was a cheerful background to our mood.

"We'll still have some time until production," I reminded Al.

Al Niemela is a hard working man. He eats and sleeps his work. His response was in character. "I'm a thousand pounds lighter. Bring it on. The cats will be ready." He turned his head toward the back of the van. "How about that, Syn? You ready to work?"

Above the singing of the tires and the thud of the rain, there rose a sound that would never tempt a choral director. It was Syn telling Al in his most positive Siamese tone that he was now ready for anything.

Bristle Face

The Film's Story

Every week for more than 25 years millions of viewers have enjoyed the national TV network program titled "The Wonderful World of Disney." *Bristle Face,* based on the book by Zachary Ball and presented on the Disney TV show, is a motion picture comedy of a bristle-faced dog who "adopts" an orphan boy.

Fourteen-year-old Jace (Phillip Alford) sets out to make his own way in the world and is soon joined by a fellow vagabond, the bristle-faced stray dog. They are befriended by an easy-going country storekeeper, Lute Swank (Brian Keith), who offers to take Jace on as a partner "to give me more thinking time to work out my problems." Lute's main concentrations are a widow, Mrs. Jarkey (Jeff Donnell), and hunting

126

with his cronies, who include Emory Packer (Wallace Ford), Newt Pribble (Slim Pickens) and Hermie (George Lindsey).

Jace longs to join the fox chases, and hopes to convert Bristle Face into a fox hunter. The dog, however, is more clown than hound — until he sees a fox on the run. His interest aroused, Bristle Face becomes the best fox hound of all.

Even though Bristle Face has learned to chase foxes, he still will not answer the hunter's horn calling him off the hunt. Because he could run himself to exhaustion, his adopted master Jace tries desperately to train him to the horn.

Bristle Face beats Sheriff Rad Toler's dog in a fight and incurs the officer's wrath. When Lute Swank stands up for the boy and his dog, he finds he has unintentionally launched his candidacy for the sheriff's office in the upcoming election. He is strongly supported by oldtimer Emory Packer, the attractive widow Jarkey and Newt Pribble.

The Training

The star of *Bristle Face* was a purebred German Wirehaired Pointer, a breed with a harsh, wiry coat and noted for its bushy eyebrows, beard and whiskers. For a change, Mr. Koehler selects an off-camera incident that involved no training and did not appear in the movie. It did involve two crossbred "extras" in the film and how one of them outran a prize-winning hound and the whole pack trained and experienced in trials.

The Amateur Beats
the Professionals

"WHICH DISNEY DOG WAS THE BEST?"

This question is often asked. I would have to answer it by saying, "Each of them for the job he was called upon to do." If the question were, "Which was the best all-round dog," the answer might be twofold: Prince and Tiger. They were brothers, and so identical in appearance that they made one character—one of the most potent characters imaginable. They were a cross between a Redbone hound and a Boxer. Any hound man would have accepted them as purebred Redbones. Not even in their typical hound heads was there any suggestion of Boxer except for slightly shorter ears. They had the size and beautiful color of the Redbones. They had perfect working dog temperaments, which gives the drive to work at full capacity and the equanimity to relax completely. The best commentary on their temperaments is made by the many things they could do perfectly.

They had graduated from a novice obedience class at eight months. Tiger placed first with 199 and Prince second with 198—the highest possible score is 200. Hal and I acquired them shortly after we came home from location on *The Incredible Journey*. Fired with success, the young couple who owned them wished to compete in obedience trials, which are open only to purebred dogs. They would trade their dogs to us for the payment for any purebred puppy they might select, and the full assurance that the "brothers" got the best of care and affection.

"You bet," Hal told them. "You pick a pup, and we'll pay for it."

We began a program of advanced training and picture patterns that would bring to light the pluses and minuses of temperament. We found no deficiencies. The pluses were many. One of the most unusual things we noticed was an enthusiasm "to do," whether the action was logically satisfying or not. Their attitude and action were as good on a slow hesitant walk or yawn as on a wild run or a jump.

Both were versatile and athletic, although Tiger was better on some actions and Prince on others. Tiger would hurl himself frantically against a closed door when cued from the opposite side. In the same situation, Prince would demonstrate less violently. Both would hit the water and swim as well as good Labradors do. In an unlimited range of actions they complemented each other perfectly. In appearance, they were so similar that they could double each other in a direct cut, which meant they could portray a character of almost unlimited ability.

Prince and Tiger were about eleven months old, and not quite through their picture training, when Hal and I were given the script for *Bristle Face*.

The dog I was to train for the title role was a German Wirehaired Pointer. One of the story points called for Bristle Face to outrun a large pack of hounds. We had the use of a top pack of hunting hounds that would run a drag track. The pack numbered twenty: one bluetick, two black and tans and the rest Walkers, white with brown markings.

"Do you suppose Prince and Tiger would run with that pack?" Hal asked me. "It'd be good experience for them, and it would add another color."

"I'll work on it," I told Hal. "The shot won't come up for at least three weeks."

A month later Prince and Tiger were part of a pack that bawled and lunged against slip ropes on the upper end of a canyon on Walt Disney's Golden Oak Ranch. Five of us braced against their frantic efforts as the dogs fought to drag us down the canyon to where the owner was blowing insults on his coon squaller. Prince and Tiger seemed as frenzied as any in the pack.

"Move Tiger farther back," I screamed at Hal above the bawling. "If he gets out in front, he might lead them off the track. He's green. He ought to follow."

I saw, rather than heard, one of the pack's owners laugh as Hal backed his way through the brush with Tiger and a tangle of four other dogs. The man who laughed had mentioned earlier that one of the hounds had won both "tree and line money" at trials and could never be outrun by a green cross breed.

George, who owned most of the dogs, blasted a final infuriating note on his coon squaller, and picked his way down the canyon floor, dragging a coon-scented drag over the rocks and brush behind him. The canyon choked down to the width of a path and ended at a bend in a shallow creek, which then angled across a brushy flat. The bedlam increased as George disappeared from sight. One of the crew signaled with a rag. We slipped the dogs.

They surged down the canyon floor with the fluid moves of a flash flood. Tiger, one of those in the rear, swung to his left and then, hampered only by the rough terrain, made his move along the edge of the pack. The canyon narrowed. Two dogs were ahead of Tiger, then only one—"the trial winner"—blocked the narrow path before him. Somehow Tiger found footing for a mighty leap that took him over the dog. Spray flew as he plowed through the creek and shot out onto the flat. It was the moment of truth. Was Tiger really running the drag set or just running? He swerved to his right to follow the same path George had taken with the drag. Tiger was not racing against the hounds. The green dog had actually beaten the trial winner and an experienced pack at their own game.

Boomerang the turkey herder.

Boomerang, Dog of Many Talents

The Film's Story

Now you might think that Boomerang is a peculiar name for a redbone hound. Unless, of course, you repeatedly sold that dog to different people all over the country, and you knew that no matter how often you sold him, he would always return to you.

Well, that is precisely what Barney Duncan (Darren McGavin), an imaginative con-man in the turn-of-the-century West, does to his pet and companion in *Boomerang, Dog of Many Talents*. This amazing adventure film appeared on "Walt Disney's Wonderful World of Color" TV show.

First Barney sells Boomerang as an Australian cattle dog to a rancher, then as a watchdog to an unscrupulous storekeeper who goes back on his word to a youngster, Simon Graham.

Meeting Simon's mother, Molly (Patricia Crowley), Barney learns that she is a widow and a turkey farmer with a flock of about 500. Molly is just getting ready to drive the "herd" to market and can use all the help she can get. Though he resists, claiming that he hates turkeys and has to be somewhere else soon, the footloose Barney is trapped into going on the 100-mile drive. The unusual turkey-herding hound manages to keep the home-grown birds in line until some wild turkeys beckon from the hillsides and all 500 gobblers make a break for it.

When Barney, Molly and the hound finally round them up, the count shows that thirty are still missing. Boomerang later locates them in the pen of a husky trapper who insists that they are his. Barney manages to retrieve the birds by trading Boomerang, "a genuine hunting dog," to the trapper for the turkeys.

Later, remaining true to his name, Boomerang eludes his now would-be owner and returns to his true master.

The Training

For the part of "Boomerang" Bill Koehler tried several herding breeds, including a Border Collie experienced in working sheep. But the Collie was frustrated because the turkeys wouldn't play the herding game.

In the following training sequence Bill tells how he and his partner suddenly got the brilliant inspiration to use Prince and Tiger, the crossbred Boxer-Redbone hounds we met in *Bristle Face*. They proved to be turkey-herding dogs of the highest caliber. Then Bill reveals how another trainer's intuition kept the hundreds of turkeys comfortable in the searing desert sun.

Prince and Tiger
Handle a Hard-Headed Herd

IT WAS *Boomerang, Dog of Many Talents* that gave Prince and Tiger the best showcase for their versatility. One of the many things that would be required of Boomerang would be that he herd turkeys. The story line was woven around driving four hundred turkeys to market. Because competent herding was essential, we turned first to dogs that had been bred for herding, even though they might not be good prospects for the other actions.

Our property department had purchased a flock of birds and placed them on a farm about ten miles from the studio, and it was there we tried the dogs. The last of the herding breeds we tried was a Border Collie, experienced in working sheep and other livestock, that had demonstrated his ability by herding and penning ducks at exhibitions. We tried him on a small group of the turkeys. They faced him like a bunch of feathered fools. Generally, when he darted in to press them, their only movement was to raise and lower their heads, or to pick at his nose when it came close enough. The dog was frustrated. A little nip to move a sheep is permissible, but just how do you nip a turkey that has never been handled by a dog, and how hard do you do it? When he sidled into them they pushed toward him and picked at his head.

"It's gonna take a dog that will slam into them a few times," Hal said. "Then maybe they'll rove."

"Tiger!" we said in unison.

There might be some way Tiger's enthusiasm would help him do the job.

The next day we were back at the turkey yard and parked near the edge of the flock. We heard our dogs thump about in their crates as they picked up the gamey scent of the birds.

Tiger came from the van with his tail and head high, looking and sniffing. His quizzical look showed he related his presence to the turkeys, but how—a chase maybe?

A half dozen of the more enterprising birds had split off from the big flock and were prospecting along the edge of a lane. I put a training collar and longe line on Tiger, which told him that there was something new to be learned. The strays moved to the far side of the road where we could start a remote pressure that would squeeze them back toward the flock. I began to work the dog toward them, changing course each time the birds probed their chances to go to the right or left. Erratically, they eased back toward the flock. My own "herding moves" and intensity had drawn Tiger a good picture. He took the initiative. Still on the longe, he moved out in front of me, reading the attitude of the birds. Handling his front feet like a cutting-horse, he turned to frustrate each bird that had a naughty thought. Then, as he moved farther out in front and monopolized all of the bird's attention, the situation changed. The turkeys were no longer moving. Tiger combined some threatening moves with explosive barks. The birds stood, ready to pick, just as they had for the experienced Border Collie.

Now it was up to Tiger. He had worked around all kinds of livestock without ever attempting to hurt any creature, so I

136

knew there was no risk in removing the longe and leaving him to solve the problems. Free of the longe, the red dog made another pass, feinting and barking furiously. No turkey moved. The dog and birds froze in a weird tableau. Suddenly, Tiger whirled away in a tight circle and came back like impending doom. His head was high as he drove his chest into one big gobbler and spun another with his shoulder. Two more pellmell charges knocked another pair of the big birds backward. The next face-off proved that the turkeys had got the message. Meekly, the rest of the strays sought the anonymity of the big flock.

Tiger strutted along the edge of the herd as though he had found a new career. He speedily thumped any strays, rolling or skidding, back into the community.

Communication is rapid among birds. Word went through the flock: "Move before you're moved."

"Let's try Prince," Hal said.

I took Prince, on the longe, along the edge of the flock until a few strays finally provided a learning situation. The turkeys had gotten the word from Tiger, and trotted back to the flock from the slightest pressure. Success taught Prince in a hurry, and we left the farm with two dogs that would herd turkeys.

The herding had been the big question. The scores of things that would be required of Boomerang could be accomplished by hard work and the ability of our red dogs. There really was a *Boomerang, Dog of Many Talents*.

Compie's Cool Turkeys

WALT DISNEY'S FANS have marvelled at the actions of the dogs, cats and wild animals in his pictures, but have generally been unaware of the skills and ingenuity needed to accomplish the scenes that feature farm animals in important roles. Nor do they know that the problems relating to the care and maintenance of featured farm animals can at times be as complex as those that relate to wild animals. Such complications can be expected in the case of a production that features turkeys; and Walt Disney's *Boomerang, Dog of Many Talents* featured over 400 of those big birds. Experienced turkey breeders said what we were about to attempt was impossible.

"If you try to move turkeys when the temperature is above ninety-six degrees, they'll pile up and smother," was the unanimous opinion.

Our story called for our big flock to make long treks behind a wagon, and lots of action when they were herded by Boomerang. At times they would have to run wildly and fly away. The location for the big scenes would be Walt's Golden Oaks Ranch on the edge of the desert. Production was scheduled for August and September when the days would be long and the sky unclouded so that the light would be abundant and uniform for filming our sea of shining turkeys. The temperature during the day would range from 100° to 115°.

138

So the problem was to do an impossible job, protect the birds and keep them comfortable. Because the job was impossible, Barney Rogers called Lionel Comport. "Compie" was literally born into the business of handling motion picture livestock. His father had been active in the field as long ago as 1925. The years Compie had spent with animals had given him an intuition that took over when mere knowledge failed.

Five months before production was to start, hundreds of turkey poults were delivered for Comport to raise and teach to follow a wagon. Shortly after that, the wagon that Pat Crowley would drive on the long trip to market was delivered. Now the world of the gangly, fuzzy-feathered poults took on another dimension. No longer did the feed they seemed always to expect come from poultry feeders. They quickly learned that each time a man appeared at the back door of the wagon, feed would come flying from his hands. The banging of the man's hand on the bucket soon brought the response of a mother hen's call to food. Their faith became such that, even when the man did not appear, they believed, when the pail was thumped, food would quickly follow the sound from the darkness of the wagon. Soon, when the thumping came while "Mother Wagon" was in motion the big family followed along trying to pass or jump over each other, convinced that "she" was calling them to where food would be more plentiful. Compie had plugged them into "Mother Wagon" in a hurry. But it was a long time from June to September. And there's a big difference between a rare June day and sizzling September. But at least they were following the wagon.

Because I needed to familiarize my dogs with the turkeys, we spent much time training on the edge of the flock; and I was able to observe the birds changing from dull poults to beautifully feathered creatures. When viewed from a distance against the green of the pasture, the light reflection from the bronze backs gave the illusion of an undulating mirror as the flock prospected across the irrigated fields.

Toward the middle of July the days suddenly grew warmer but the turkeys were as active as ever. August brought another big rise in temperature.

Early in the morning of the first day of production we knew it was going to be stifling hot. Any night chill and moisture were already gone from the ground. While we had our coffee and doughnuts beneath a big tree near the trucks, the sun rose above the hills to the east and snuffed out the last of the morning freshness. The sun would have to do a lot more climbing before the light would be right on the entire stretch of road our first travel shot would cover.

During the morning we shot close-ups of Darren McGavin and Boomerang on and around the wagon. The increase in temperature was marked by the number of times the makeup man mopped the perspiration from Darren's face. Between takes the crew made a steady run on the water cooler and salt tablets. As he drank, each person looked over to where Compie and his men were holding the turkeys for the afternoon's big shot. There were no open mouths or other signs to show that the birds minded the heat.

Immediately after lunch the wagon was placed for the start of a shot and the turkeys were moved into position to follow the sound of the pail that would come from the wagon. Boomerang would trail behind the flock, ready to head off any birds that sought to explore the roadside brush. An American Humane Association man would be in position to watch for any adverse effect the heat might have on the birds. At the first sign of discomfort to the turkeys, we would stop the shot.

Finally, the big shot was organized, and a megaphone boomed "Action." The wagon rumbled forward, and from its interior came the thumping on the pail. Big toms gobbled excitedly from various places in the flock and the big bronze mass surged after the wagon. By halfway point none of the turkeys had broken ranks in favor of the nearby shade trees. The Humane Association man and all of us watched closely. The birds seemed only concerned with the sound that came from the wagon.

The megaphone boomed "Cut," and the shot ended. The turkeys milled around the wagon expressing faith that the sound they had followed meant food. Their manna came by the bucket, bouncing like hail off the hard backs of the faithful.

Compie grinned while he watched them eat.

During the hot weeks and the big shots that followed, our turkeys continued to be indifferent to the heat; and Comport continued to grin mysteriously. The *Los Angeles Times* and other papers in the area gave accounts of whole flocks of turkeys being lost. What had been a concern became more and more a mystery. Something about our birds was different. And Comport continued to grin.

On a blistering hot day toward the end of our picture, some difficulties with close-ups prevented us from getting to a big afternoon shot with the turkeys as we had planned. All day the birds had been held in portable enclosures. When it was certain that there would be no time to use them, it was cleared for the wranglers to take the turkeys back to the night pens near the ranch house. Compie and two of his men jerked the holding pens open, and a flood of birds swept across the field. Suddenly, like a covey of bob white quail, they flared up in a short flight, landed and then took off again. All of us stood silently watching as our turkeys, of their own volition, expressed their total indifference to the heat that was destroying thousands of their kind on poultry ranches. It was quite a sight. Comport grinned wider than ever.

"How did you do it, Compie?" I asked.

Without any discourses on such things as calories or metabolism, I got the answer.

"I took them off all grain before the picture started, except for the little we used to bait them. They've been getting nothing but green stuff off that irrigated field."

Those Calloways

The Film's Story

Based on the book "Stillwater" by Paul Annixter, *Those Calloways* brings to the screen a hearty slice of New England life with warmth, humor and universality. It is a beautiful story, beautifully filmed, and the kind of outdoor drama that is right down the Disney alley.

The stars — Brian Keith, Vera Miles, Brandon de Wilde, Walter Brennan and Ed Wynn — bring to life the backwoods Calloway family, and the small town folks in Swiftwater, Vermont. The stirring tale is about a simple woodsman and his proud family who put everything they own on the block to protect the great flocks of wild geese that cross their sky.

The Calloways are characters, normally, with a 500-pound bear in the cellar, a loud-mouthed crow in the kitchen, and a

143

The Calloway family fought to save the beautiful Canada geese.

Brandon de Wilde watches "Keg" come out of hibernation.

lop-eared hound dog who doesn't know when to stop chasing a deadly wolverine.

Despite many setbacks, including an effort by a scheming promoter to convert Swiftwater into a resort for shooting wild geese, the Calloways' dream for a wild goose sanctuary is finally realized.

The Training

Once again Bill Koehler called upon the versatile crossbred Redbone hounds, Prince and Tiger, to perform for the part of the dog "Sounder." As in other Disney films featuring animals, Prince and Tiger were "doubles" for each other. In the next two accounts, Bill relates the indomitable courage and happy spirit with which these short-haired canines from sunny California adapted to the below-zero temperature and deep snow of a Vermont winter; and how his associate trainers, Lloyd Beebe and Al Niemela, achieved the "impossible" feat of staging a violent struggle between Bucky Calloway (Brandon de Wilde) and the deadly wolverine.

Short Haired Prince and Tiger
In Snow and Sub-Zero Cold

MY PARTNER and I had been convinced that Prince and Tiger could do anything a picture dog could be asked to do. We had no doubts. Then they handed us the script for *Those Calloways.*

It was not that the actions were too difficult for our dogs to perform. But, as the two dogs alternated in the role of Sounder, they would do most of their acting in deep snow while we would be rehearsing and handling on snowshoes some distance away so that the sets would remain unmarked until photographed. The location would be in Vermont's snow belt in the beautiful area near Jeffersonville. The temperature would be far below zero.

Some of the scenes called for relaxed companionship including stay-positions on the snow. The least unnaturalness would rob such scenes of their realism. How relaxed and natural would a short haired dog from Southern California be in such situations? Would there be problems in the hours of waiting in the cold between scenes? We would use furniture pads to cover our crates. But how would a dog, coming from comparative warmth of a crate, portray a delicate attitude when hit with a massive temperature change?

It was warm and sunny when we watched our dogs being loaded carefully into our plane's cargo bay for the flight to New York. It was warm on the plane. There was only a hint of chill as we left the plane in New York and the winter coats on the passengers in the warm terminal seemed as strange as the ones we carried over our arms. It was a bit cooler on the shuttle flight to Vermont. An hour later we taxied to the docking area in front of the Burlington terminal. Our plane was an older piston engine twin with a loading ramp that lowered directly under the tail section. The ramp went down and the cold came up. Blue cold. Maintenance had removed nearly all of the snow from the airport and formed it into hills and crags around its perimeter. We watched as our crates were taken from the baggage compartment and lowered to the ground. We opened the doors, and the dogs came out into a 25 below zero temperature.

If our dogs felt any shock from the cold, it wasn't evident. They revelled in the opportunity of exercising along the airport's wall of snow. There was no shivering nor raising of a foot free of the frozen ground.

"There wasn't time for the cold to sink in yet," Hal said as we loaded our dogs and gear into the station wagon which had been rented for us.

It was an hour across a masterpiece of moonlight and snow to Jeffersonville. The snow seemed twice the height of a car as we turned into the drive that led from the road to the cleared area in front of our motel. Our unit manager had reserved the entire facility for our company. Thanks to our host, Bill Kenny, housing in the comfortable basement had been provided for our dogs. The fox, wolverines and other animals Lloyd Beebe had brought from Washington were suitably quartered in a cooler part of the basement.

The following morning as we descended the basement stairs the sounds of scuffling feet and busy tails told us our dogs were rested and ready. A door at the rear of the basement led to a stairway that climbed steeply up to the ground level and another door that was slanted for better opening when the snow was deep. We took our dogs through the first doorway and closed the door behind us and felt a temperature that warned us of what lay beyond the second door. This slanted door gave easily to our upward thrust, and we found that it and the paved area around it had been cleared of snow. At the edge of the pavement, a telephone pole protruded from seven feet of snow. Nearby, a small tree held its lower limbs a few inches above the white blanket.

"They'll do for quick tie-outs," Hal said. We fastened a long tie-chain to the pole and another to the tree. It is a way of telling a picture dog, "This is the time and the place," instead of letting him make such a decision when he's working free before the camera. Several of our company on the way to and from vehicles stopped to see how the bitter cold would affect the dogs. A typical comment was: "Wait'll they're out in it a while—they'll wish they were back in California."

With tails wagging enthusiasm and muzzles probing snow to eye level, our dogs seemed unaware of what the cold should do to them. They were still enchanted by a world that was fresh, white, and cold when we crunched our way back to the basement stairs.

"Let's go get some breakfast," Hal said. "Ham and hot-cakes with Vermont maple syrup. Then we can mount those snowshoes and start working out some of our problems."

One of the problems shared by all our company was that of keeping the virgin snow unmarked. Tracks, other than those made by our cast, would destroy the wilderness effect.

There could be no rehearsals on the sets, nor second takes. Norman Tokar, our director, would have to prepare each sequence away from the set and then give any further instructions with a bull horn. Many times our dog would be working so far from his trainer that he would be practically a free agent. The only solution would be to hold him in proper orientation to the actor. On this, we would need help.

Fortified with a heavy breakfast, we took advantage of the white fields adjacent to the motel to give our dogs their introduction to the universal joy that all animals experience when they are first exposed to snow. They sank belly deep in the fluffy stuff but, with the undulating gait like short legged weasels, were able to run ecstatic zigzag courses in all directions.

The dashes were interspersed with sudden stops and eardeep thrusts of the head as though to peer into another world from which the joy might be coming. Each time the head went down, the tail pointed up at the dark sky. Occasionally, they would pause and stare at us as though wondering why we didn't understand about snow. The cold and snow, at least in short exposures and while they were active, caused our dogs no discomfort. But there was another problem. Some of the exterior scenes were a very serious and somber part of our story. We knew that the novelty of the snow would end. And there would have to be a further change in attitude. For the Calloways' dog to be happy during the family's troubles would contradict the mood.

It took about a half hour for our dogs' ecstasy to subside. We put a long light line on each dog, and without a word of command, started snowshoeing across the field in opposite directions, Hal with Prince and I with Tiger. Every time a dog's attention strayed, the handler turned sharply so that he came

150

Sounder protests being tied up outside the labyrinth.

Sounder catches a scent.

up solid against the line. Because of a good foundation of obedience training, they soon settled into a pattern that was casual but so well oriented that the line could no longer surprise them. Both dogs took the pattern rapidly, but Prince looked better in the role of "a close companion" for the traveling shots. He held a tighter pattern than his brother did and each time Hal paused to catch his breath, Prince stood casually near him. We moved aimlessly across the fields for a little longer in a wind that numbed our faces and made talk difficult. There was still no sign of discomfort in our dogs.

Hal snowshoed up to me and yelled through stiff lips, "Let's go in for a while."

In the warmth of the motel's lobby we drank coffee and discussed our findings. It appeared that the only effect the cold had on our dogs, at least when they were moving, was to exhilarate them.

"Whichever one we use, he'll need some preliminary work off to one side of every shot so he doesn't go into it feeling too high," Hal said.

"It'll take a lot of work before and during production," I agreed. "And it must be with a stranger—we've got to wean them away from us. We've got to have a stranger to send them with."

Brandon de Wilde, a principal in our picture who liked dogs, had offered to help us, but we knew his time would be limited.

The problem of a capable stranger was solved the next morning. We were in the lobby when a young man in heavy woolens identical to those Brandon would wear in the traveling shots, entered the room. From snatches of conversation, we gathered that his name was Jim and he would double for Brandon in some far shots. He was a ski instructor.

"I'll have some time and I like dogs," he said.

"Now's a good time," Hal said.

Jim followed us down the inside stairway to where our dogs thumped a welcome from their crates. He admired each in turn as they responded to his greeting.

"They look great. But with that short coat don't they . . .?"

I raised my hand. "No, they don't. They just get happy."

"Yeah," Hal added, "We want them happy. We just don't want them to show it at the wrong time. That's why we're hoping you can help us."

A week later, Prince, no longer trailing a short line, would cue from Jim's moves each time he changed direction. Tiger was slightly less responsive. In the few periods that Brandon was able to work with the dogs, he was delighted to find the dogs equally interested in him.

There were many things that the role of Sounder required besides holding position in the big traveling shots. Some scenes required him to remain at rest in temperatures far below zero. In rehearsals, the dogs showed no more discomfort outdoors than if they had been on a living room rug.

By the time production started, members of our company no longer asked whether cold bothered our dogs. But the question came from another quarter. Sometimes there would be visitors to our locations, standing between the sets and where our vehicles were parked. Disney Production people appreciate and enjoy the friendship of the areas where we work. We answer many questions about Walt Disney Productions and our dedication to good family entertainment.

"How do your dogs stand the cold?" was the question Hal and I were asked most often while we were in Vermont.

Against the logistic problems of Vermont's coldest winter in over a half century, we used coke pots to keep our cameras operable, to offset rehearsals for our scenes, and to stay close to schedule. Newspaper people in the region visited us often to observe the difficulty of doing the big snow scenes. One of their stories expressed surprise that the Disney crew seemed to be unaffected by the cold. It mentioned further that our short haired dogs seemed to mind the cold less than did the local dogs.

I can still see our shiny red dogs undulating across snow fields against the background of the Green Mountains. It's easy to recall the smell of the cold and feel the wind stinging tears from my eyes as I watched the dogs suddenly stop so that they might feel the magic press in on them from all directions. If you were to ask me to say under oath why the dogs were so at home in the severe cold, there is only one answer I could give you. It was for the same reason they could stand long runs in extreme heat, rushing water and other stresses, and do so many things that would stump other dogs. It was because they were Prince and Tiger.

Brandon battles the wolverine.

It's a Long Way to a Wolverine's Heart

HOW DOES a motion picture animal trainer cope when he is asked to do something that conventional knowledge suggests is impossible? He does it. By creating a necessity to succeed, motion pictures have caused trainers to explore and develop approaches to animals working at liberty that would be foreign to the experimental psychologist whose conclusions are reached in the restricted environment of a laboratory.

Walt Disney created an interesting training problem in his production, *Those Calloways*. The story called for a violent struggle between a man and a mature wolverine. The animal was to be in full possession of all its faculties—no sedating, no muzzling.

Lloyd Beebe and Al Niemela of the Olympic Game Farm in Sequim, Washington were asked to find and train the animal.

Lloyd is a compact, powerful man with amazing balance and agility, whether he's wearing logging boots or showshoes. None of his physical abilities surprises me since I saw him, camera and tripod in hand, jump off the edge of a railroad trestle and land lightly on the end of a joist protruding four feet below the ties and seventy-five feet above a rocky creek. If Lloyd has nerves, they're awfully good.

Al Niemela, a blue eyed Finn, has long worked at training animals ranging from chipmunks to bears, and most creatures in between. He has patience, ingenuity and an interest that have brought him great insight into animal character. It is said that Al would cheerfully be eaten by a bear if it meant a chance to study the bear's interior.

Al and Lloyd had worked with wolverines before, but not in such a demanding situation as they now faced. To teach isolated routines or patterns where a wolverine did not interact with a person is one thing; to condition such an animal to understand and accept the physical contact and moves of a "wrestling" man as posing no threat would be quite another.

The wolverine is the most unweasel-like member of his family. He smells strong and he is strong. The weasel, ferret and mink earn their living by stealth, cunning and a small size that helps them to enter anything from a rabbit's burrow to a chicken coop. The wolverine lives by frontal assault, although there are some who have witnessed incidents that suggest his courage is unpredictable.

Pat Wayne, the star of Disney's *The Bears and I,* had an experience that supports this belief. Pat, whose affection for the bear cubs in the picture was returned fully by the cubs, was to walk into a scene, accompanied by the little bears, where a wolverine was eating a meal on a stump. One of the cubs spotted the gorging animal from a distance. With a vocal threat and a pell-mell charge, the cub chased the wolverine into the woods.

Lloyd Beebe believes that it is the wolverine's instinctive knowledge of leverage and mechanics, as much as his phenomenal strength that enables him to rob caches and vandalize cabins.

Lloyd and others who know the wolverine agree that there

is no assurance in the animal's unpredictable character and that his strength and agility are very real.

It is seldom practical to schedule a motion picture so that an animal can be raised to maturity by the time he will be needed. The first task was to find a wild, adult wolverine. Among the candidates that had been captured in Canada, all snarled their opinion of the man who studied them, but Lloyd chose one as a slightly better prospect than the others. He named him Joey.

The production schedule had been set. The wolverine had to be ready. The training must proceed as rapidly as possible, without risking mistakes and setbacks. A man would have to live with Joey almost constantly. Lloyd and Al decided to take twelve-hour shifts. Each was to depend on his own observations. Until a much later date there would be no further discussion of failure or progress. To share experiences too early might curb initiative.

Joey's "den," a crate where he slept and sought seclusion when anyone approached his pen, was taken to a comfortable room in a barn, and its door propped open.

During the first twelve hour shift, Joey's scent and growl filled the room as he glowered at Al from the darkness of his den. Toward the end of the day, the growls were a bit more mechanical than emotional.

The man's only offense was being alive. Al had no more emotion than the chair, the cot or the walls. His first significant move came later in the day when he tossed a piece of meat onto the feeding board near the crate. Joey's reaction was to growl more intensely at the move. He showed no interest in the meat.

Joey growled with all his earlier intensity as the shift ended and a new man entered. He saw the same indifference in this man as in the first and again his growls subsided to mere mechanics. He huffed a couple of times as the man laid down on a mattress about six feet away and turned on a transistor radio.

In the way that all living things know about life, Joey knew when the man fell asleep. There were no thoughts, attitudes nor actions to concern him. Joey stopped growling.

For three weeks, Joey flashed out from the crate to grab his food during the few minutes both men were out of the room at the change of a shift. He would back into the seclusion of the crate with the generous slabs of meat, to eat unobserved. Then one day he grabbed his food as Al opened the door to leave. A few days later, Al placed the meat with a pole. Joey stared a moment at the new thing, then, with Al watching, grabbed the meat and backed into the crate. A week later, he growled a warning and grabbed the meat from the pole while Al retained his grip. The pole became more and more familiar—and each day it became an inch shorter.

Joey learned to enjoy his meals even when a man was present and talking. Soon the pole was about three inches long and the meat was against Al's hand. One day, Al did not extend the meat. He sat flat on the floor and held it over his leg. There was no way for Joey to reach the food without putting his feet on Al's leg. Al's carefully calculated moves convinced Joey that the man's leg, even when moving, was no threat.

It was about that time that Lloyd and Al compared their experiences in handling Joey. In turn, each described every step he had taken. From the first tossed meat through the gradual shortening of the poles, their steps had paralleled in a way that was eerie. They were equal in their understanding of the wolverine and the progress they had made. They were ready to go to the next step in the socialization of Joey.

160

Many times, in training an animal, it is essential to have one trainer practice the actor's role while another trainer concentrates on placing and handling the animal in relation to him. Lloyd would be going on location and probably double the actor, so it was logical that he be the one to show Joey that body contact and quick moves meant food and friendship, not threats.

Joey glowered and growled as he watched Lloyd start the new level of training by lying flat on his back. He watched suspiciously as Al placed a piece of meat on Lloyd's chest. In the way of the wolverine, he froze; his stare was cold and unblinking. Lloyd was equally still during the long wait until Joey finally took the meat from his chest, and scuttled backward to eat it.

Gradually, over a period of weeks, Lloyd introduced motion into the training sessions. He moved his body, arms and legs in ways that were always preliminary to a stillness which gave Joey a chance to get his meat. In Lloyd's mind none of the motions were addressed to Joey, and before long the wolverine would thrust against or under a moving arm.

Joey grew more and more encouraged by the movements that told him there was meat to be found on Lloyd's thrashing body. There were no brain waves that related to fear or suspicion for the wolverine to sense.

The men staged training situations with distractions in other parts of the barn, so that Joey would become accustomed to the changes in environment. But there was one change they could not accustom him to: actual production.

Seventeen hundred miles from where he had lived as a suspicious wild wolverine, a fascinated production crew watched Joey crouch on Lloyd Beebe's chest. The set was a simulated log jam. The smells of the stage, the sounds, and the staring humans were light years from the freshness of moist earth, the wind in the trees and the chuckling of a stream. It was all very strange to Joey.

There was a soft "Action!" from the Director.

Joey turned his unfathomable eyes to the subdued activity near the camera. Lloyd rocked his body a bit and the wolverine turned his attention back to the man lying beneath him. Lloyd began to hump and roll. Now there was something familiar to Joey. He shoved his way through the barrier of arms toward the man's throat. Violently, Lloyd opposed him. Joey shoved furiously against the restraining arms. The action was that of a death struggle.

"Cut." The word released enthusiastic comments from all who had watched. One "take" was sufficient.

Many behavioral scientists would minimize the chances of bringing an adult, wild wolverine to the point of reliable performance under stage conditions. But the understanding and delicacy with which Lloyd related to Joey was not science. It was art—art and something else.

That Darn Cat

The Film's Story

One of the funniest of all Disney productions, *That Darn Cat* features such great Hollywood talents as Hayley Mills, Dean Jones, Dorothy Provine, Roddy McDowall, Ed Wynn and Elsa Lanchester.

In the story, adapted from the book "Undercover Cat" by the Gordons, a slippery Siamese named D. C. — short for Darn Cat — picks up the only clue to a bank robbery when a kidnapped lady teller slips her wrist watch around his neck. Since D. C. can't tell the F. B. I. where he's been, they have to follow him and hope he returns to the criminals' lair.

This proves a mite more difficult than one would expect, since cats are smaller and faster than cops, and D. C. is a gregarious sort whose evening rounds include raiding kitchens

A cat burglar steals a duck.

An enraged Roddy McDowall trips over a sprinkler and D.C. carries his stolen duck over the man's prostrate body.

This is hardly what the patrons expected
to see on the screen of a drive-in movie.

and garbage cans up and down alleys, swiping a neighbor's roast duck, cadging handouts at a drive-in theater, and disappearing under fences. Finally the Federal Security agent places a transmitter "bug" under D. C.'s collar and follows the cat to the crooks' apartment. D. C. "catches" one of the crooks by tripping him on the stairs and the agents complete the arrests.

For the title role, Disney chose Syn, the Siamese who starred in *The Incredible Journey*. Syn won the coveted Patsy Award for Best Animal Actor for his performance in *That Darn Cat*.

The Training

Trainer Bill Koehler describes in the next three chapters how he and Al Niemela set up various intricate signaling devices to guide Syn into the difficult actions the script called for. Animal trainers must possess amazing powers of ingenuity in suiting the natural behavior of their stars to perfect on-camera performance.

Haley Mills wonders why her cat is wearing a wrist watch.

Haley Mills and Dean Jones try to send a message through the transmitter in D.C.'s collar.

D.C. says he's against being paw printed.

Haley Mills and Dean Jones get D.C.'s paw prints on more than the paper.

"A Cat's in Business For Himself"
—True or False?

"A cat's in business for himself."

This statement by Jimmy Woods, a philosophical "sound man," does not necessarily support the popular belief that the training of a domestic cat is limited to a "bait job" or to the conditioning of responses solely through the use of food reinforcement. Cat lovers, with puzzling pride, have long been selling their pets short with statements that a cat is totally independent and does only what he wants to do. Other than using bribery, they have done little to make a cat "want to do" the right things. With those who have sold the cat short, and particularly Skinnerians and others who have deified the Conditioned Reflex Box, I share some facts that might disquiet you.

Walt Disney began the production of *That Darn Cat* on October 9, 1964 and, with the exception of a little extra second unit work with untrained kittens, finished on December 30th. Eleven weeks. The next time you see the picture, count the number of definable actions and attitudes that the cat portrays. You'll be convinced that the wonderful little animal did many intricate things and with perfect accuracy and timing.

Syn, who starred in *The Incredible Journey*, was cast in the role of D.C. He and one double did ninety percent of the work.

This work was not done in an experimental psychologist's laboratory. The cats were subjected to all of the challenges and distractions of the sets and to the limitless space of the back lot. Obviously, the cats had something going for them besides the food reinforcement which we sometimes used during the early stages of training.

Syn and his doubles had been seasoned on *The Incredible Journey,* but each picture brings new and unique problems. The cat that had performed so superbly in relationship to the wilderness and other animals, with only a few scenes with humans, would now have to interact with Haley Mills, Dean Jones, Dorothy Provine and other members of a large featured cast. And the script called for many close and medium shots that would require absolute precision. The complexity of lighting some of the scenes would require a forest of lights and screens limiting the spots where I could work.

There was a greater problem. The effective but cumbersome equipment we had used on *The Incredible Journey* would be almost unusable in the jungle of light standards, props and people. A change from our cord-activated release box and our swinging sheep bell was needed. But Syn was so familiar with the tone and inflection of our bell that a change to something like an electric buzzer might require weeks of orientation. There was indeed a problem. If Syn were to fail in his timing, a highly paid human actor would be dangling actions and dialogue in a senseless space. And production was scheduled to begin.

Walt Disney's huge Stage 4, when not being used for production, is a good place to wrestle with problems. With the doors closed, a lone work light is as a candle would be in an immense cave. Some of the sets we would use on our picture had already been built on the stage. So, in addition to the welcome seclusion for planning, there was an opportunity to anticipate some of the geography of the scenes.

It was on Stage 4 that Art Vitarelli and I first discussed the "problem of the bell."

It is more than a heritage of Italian genius that would make Art able to understand immediately any problem ever faced by Leonardo da Vinci, Joe DiMaggio and His Holiness, Pope Paul. Not large in physical stature, Art is many times larger than most men in creative ability. From an early background that included commercial photography, professional ice skating and various jobs in motion picture production, Art's native perceptiveness had been developed to a point where he understands all facets of film making and how they can be reconciled to each other. At Disney's and, in the world at large, he is unique.

Now, Art watched Syn come out of my cord-controlled release box and go unerringly to the source of the bell's signal. "Would he go to a recording of the bell?" he asked.

"Possible," I answered. "Most voices are changed so much by transcription that they don't sound natural to animals. Most of the cases where an animal supposedly identifies his master's transcribed voice blow up when you test them. But let's give it a try."

Art went to the stage phone that stood on a nearby pedestal. Shortly, a man from the Sound Department brought a tape recorder and some other equipment. While Art placed the recorder and mike, I took Syn out to my van. I didn't want to extinguish his willingness by letting him hear the bell when he couldn't respond to it.

"All set," Art said when I rejoined him.

I rang the bell with the rhythm pattern that had called the cat infallibly all through the filming of *The Incredible Journey*.

When we finished recording, Art reversed the tape for playback. He attached a speaker core to the sound outlet. The Vitterelli conception was now evident. The core was only two inches in diameter and an inch thick. Attached to a long, light wire, there was hardly a limit on where it could be placed. Under clothing, within furniture, behind a lamp—the possibilities were boundless. Free at last! But only if Syn would identify the recorded sound. I trotted off the stage to get him.

As part, and only a part, of his early training, Syn had received food rewards at the bell. If he needed confirmation of the transcribed sound, sight and taste might be helpful. I put a bit of meat of the face of the speaker core which Art had placed on a low box. I moved the release box back about six feet from where the sound would occur.

"That's long enough for a try," I told Art.

Art started the playback and increased the volume from a faint tinkle to the familiar sound level of the bell. I pulled the cord on the trip box for Syn's first run of the day. He came out, and paused for just a moment for a casual check of the strange environment. Then, with that deliberate trot that was singularly his, he went toward the one familiar thing in the area: the sound.

"Let's go again," Art said.

On the second run, Syn went from the box to the tiny speaker core as directly as he had gone to the moving ewe bell.

In animals as in humans there are two facets to the performance of hearing. There is the ability to hear a sound and the ability to tell instantly where the sound is coming from. We changed the positions of the release box and the sound source, and varied the volume. Neither habit nor memory of a previous pattern affected Syn. Each time he left the box he headed unerringly for the tiny speaker core.

Syn seemed to enjoy the mood of success as he rode on my shoulder to the exercise pen that had been placed for his comfort just off-stage.

Our next session brought more evidence of Art's genius. He had added new equipment. Now, instead of running it directly to the core, he attached the sound wire to a small console that was about the size of a large cigar box. There were three outlet posts on the side of the console so that wires could connect it with three speaker cores. On top was an off-on switch, a volume control, and a selector for switching from one station to another. Nearby, stood a comfortable release box with a spring-loaded door. The door was held shut against the tension of the springs by electro-magnets which could be released from a distance, causing the door to snap open. Made to Art's specifications by the Special Effects Department, the box had been crafted with much of the same beautiful precision that made Lincoln and other automated characters at Disneyland.

We could now hope to take full advantage of Syn's great ability. We could start him and signal him promptly and accurately from one spot to another, or have him pause, pleased and waiting for good things to occur.

A trainer can not completely anticipate, nor condition an animal for, every demand of action and environment that a film might require. The clutter of light standards and cables, the heat, the whir of the motors that raise and lower the arcs, and the heavy slam of the magnetic switches that turn them on and off can hardly be approximated during training. The monsterlike moves of a dollying camera, the markers or "sticks" that index a piece of film and synchronized the sound for the editor and the startling silence that precedes a director's call for "action"—all add to the environment that is uniquely "production." It is an environment that has almost everything needed to test the emotional stability of an animal.

Syn had experienced some of these things on *The Incredible Journey,* but that picture had required a minimum of interaction with humans, and then only on simple sets. Now in the pressure of pivotal interior scenes, he would need to adjust and respond to the persons and moves of a large cast.

Syn had worked his purr and push magic on everyone he met on *The Incredible Journey.* I hoped that he could do the same on his new job. Above all, there must be a real show of affection for Haley, which would depend a great deal on her attitude toward him.

All of John Mills' family are interested in animals, and Haley was most cooperative. Time after time she held and carried Syn in her arms during long rehearsals or cradled him in her lap when sitting. When a rehearsal was finished, she would give him a bit of warm attention before leaving him. Within a few days, there was no interruption in his purring when he was handed to Haley. He would knead on her arm with his front feet and give her an occasional dog-like lick on the wrist. When the position of Haley's head permitted, he would enthusiastically shove his own head against her neck and chin. When on her lap, he would settle down as if he had found a permanent home. When a rehearsal demanded, he would stay in her vicinity as though there was no place else in the world, until a cue signaled him away. Even in the rehearsal of some big scenes on Haley's bed, it was as though such action were a routine part of his life.

It was getting very easy to believe that Syn was Haley Mills' Darn Cat.

The first day of production is always an event. The active set is now completely furnished. The Director and Set Decorator make a last check to see that everything is the way it should be established.

The camera is in position for the first shot. Stand-ins inch and sidestep around the set at the direction of the camera man who is taking some last readings.

Syn had done one shot, a simple, unrehearsed run-through on a dimly lighted set. Now he was in the release box, hopefully ready for the test of a big, complex scene with Haley Mills and Dorothy Provine. Haley and Dorothy were seated at a table, which was dressed to show that they had just completed breakfast. Their long dialogue had been rehearsed to its full potential. The Director, Bob Stevenson, nodded his readiness.

"Light the arcs."

There was a series of metallic thuds from heavy switches as each arc added its bit to the light and heat.

"Put us on a bell," Joe, the First Assistant, called out.

A big doorbell sound brought an explosive silence to the stage; snuffed out all other noises on the stage.

"Ready?" Joe asked the operator.

"Ready," came the reply.

"Roll it."

"We're rolling."

One of the camera crew moved out swiftly into camera focus and clacked the markers.

"Speed," the operator called out.

Expensive cast, big crew, complex sets. Walt Disney was betting a lot of money that the cat he had named would come out of the box and walk across the table, pause near Dorothy Provine, then leisurely settle down with Haley Mills. This, the first of many intricate scenes that would call for perfect timing, could do much to win the empathy of our cast and crew, which would be so helpful to our work. To Art Vitarelli and me, the seconds were like a count-down for a space launch. We were about to see either rainbows or clouds.

"Action," the Director said.

The silence was massive. Then a click came from the release box. A second later, Syn jumped onto the table top and sauntered to the first sound cue. The sound moved from the first unit to the one near the table's edge. Syn ambled past the dishes and stopped with interest in front of Dorothy. Art switched the console to the third station, and the sound came from beneath Haley's blouse. Syn moved with the cue and settled luxuriously on the lap of the girl he had come to love.

All of us looked forward to the weeks of work ahead and saw "rainbows."

D.C. Eludes the F.B.I. Agents

IT WAS early twilight when the stray cat streaked out of the barn and ran headlong into a horseshoe stake. A resounding "pong" told of the force of the contact but the cat resumed his flight and deftly wiggled through the stock fence that blocked his path. Why the cat had chosen that moment to leave the darkness of the barn and be further frightened by the group of us that lounged on the grass near the horseshoe court was a puzzle. Why he had run into the stake was even more of a puzzle. Many years later, and two thousand miles from the old barn, thoughts of the erratic cat were brought back to me on Walt Disney's Stage 4. Dean Jones, an F.B.I. agent in *That Darn Cat,* had instructed his subordinates to keep "D.C." and the cat's tiny transmitter under close surveillance. The scene was staged in an alley that featured back fences, garbage cans, and the rears of buildings. A rainspout came down from the eave of one building and then elbowed out in a way that would discharge rain into the alley. It was in this elbow that D.C. was to hide while the F.B.I. men stood on each side of the spout and surveyed all of the environs in the most dramatic and classical style.

At a moment when their backs were turned to the spout, D.C. was supposed to emerge and streak, unseen, across the alley, and disappear before the agents turned toward the path of his flight. The coordination between agents and the cat had to be perfect or the shot would be without punch. The back of the spout had been cut so that D.C. could be placed comfortably in position for the moment when he would rocket from the spout. Much of the timing would depend on the cat's instant response, and the Director asked if we wanted to rehearse.

"We won't need a rehearsal," I told him confidently. "When you're ready, let's go for a take."

I took position with the speaker core across the alley and faced the spout. My partner was equally confident as he placed D.C. in the spout and moved swiftly out of camera.

On "action" there was a preliminary scene when the two F.B.I. agents faced each other. Then they turned away. It was my cue. I pressed the button with a rhythm that had always brought D.C. in a wild charge. A head was thrust from the spout, then D.C. emerged and walked slowly toward me. He was still in the shot and completely invisible to the agents when they turned to face each other again. We didn't need the absolute silence to tell us we'd blown it. D.C. made the same slow exit during two more takes. The silence grew heavier as all who had seen his usual response stood bewildered. We tried a short run from our trip box to the sound. He ran with his usual speed. Whatever slowed him had to do with the spout.

Hal Driscoll finally broke the silence. "Let's hang a little light bulb down in the pipe."

It was something to try. Quickly, an electrician dangled a small bulb down into the spout to just above the elbow.

When we were all in our places, I saw the Director look at his watch. Without doubt he had thought to be finished with such a simple scene within a few minutes. Now what had appeared simple seemed hopeless.

"He'll go this time," Hal said.

There were many in the crew who didn't seem to share his optimism as we got ready for the roll.

Again, on the word "action" the agents turned away from each other. I pressed the button. D.C. shot out of the spout and across the alley in three long bounds.

"Cut and print it," the Director said.

Hal had been right. Suddenly the answer to my question of long ago came to me. A cat's eye reaction to a light change was slower than we had realized. And in the midst of that change, he couldn't see clearly. I now knew why the cat that ran from the old barn had hit the horseshoe stake.

Dean Jones explains the mission to his co-agent.

Dean Jones tells his fellow agents that D.C. is one of their informants.

Teaching D.C. to Zero
in on a Hidden Sound

NOT ALL of *That Darn Cat's* moving scenes permitted the speaker core to direct him to a very obvious object such as a piece of furniture. Some parts required that he go to an exact place on a lawn or another surface that was indistinguishable from its surroundings. One such spot was on the lawn at the house of D.C.'s girl friend where he would stop and settle down with great dignity, to bask in the admiration of the beautiful Persian who watched from her place at the window. There could be no speaker core in sight, but possibly the cat might be able to beam in to a sound that came from under the turf, if the sound was not diffused nor distorted by the cover. Art Vitarelli and I had marvelled at D.C.'s orientation to a signal when the core was concealed in various places and covered by fabric, but we had yet to check on his ability to go directly to a sound muffled by something solid.

The carpenter shop made me a six-foot square platform of plywood. Its top was only two inches above the floor. It stood on sides that were solid and tightly attached all around. There would be just enough room for a speaker core and wires to be moved around beneath it.

It would serve as a riser over which turf or grass mats could be spread to match a lawn.

I loaded everything needed for the test into my van and headed for the quiet of Stage 3. I parked on the stage and closed the massive door to the sounds of the outside world. To get the most definite reading from the test, I placed the core under one corner of the riser, so that if the cat should head for the middle, I would know that he was merely centering on a "thing" where the noise originated, instead of orienting to the exact source. If he did go directly to the corner, it meant that he was going to the sound, not to something he saw in the general direction of the sound. It would mean that a cat's phenomenal orientation could somehow unscramble sounds that were muffled and distorted.

I paced off thirty feet and faced the cat's trip box toward the riser. D.C. had been trained in such a way that he would respond to his signal without any preliminary baiting or food rewards, so I was able to try him "cold." I took my position behind the trip box and started the tape. When I pushed the console button a sound came from the riser that seemed far off and different than anything I had ever heard. I squeezed the switch in my hand prayerfully.

The trip box opened and D.C. trotted thirty feet to a spot over the speaker core as though guided by a trolley. I dropped a piece of meat on the focal spot, and stood by while he chewed, purred and growled at the same time.

I put D.C. back in the box and moved the core under another corner of the riser. The stage was inactive, and there was a stack of furniture mats stored against the wall. I took one of them and spread it over the riser. This time when I pushed the console button the sound that came through the mat was so weak and diffused it was unearthly. There seemed no way of knowing where it originated. How would a cat be able to know? I pressed the trip switch. Without the slightest deviation toward where he had picked up the meat, D.C. went straight to a spot above the speaker. He had heard the sound precisely, and its pull was stronger than the previous pattern. How different than the performance of a trained retriever who, if a little weak on taking directions, would go back to the place of a previous "find."

D.C.'s ability meant we could make a buried speaker core work for our lawn shots and for any scene where the device had to be hidden beneath sound-muffling cover. Once again our work in making pictures had uncovered a fact about an animal that otherwise might not be known.

Because of our cat's phenomenal orientation to the little speaker cores, we were able to motivate and direct him to any spot where we could make a set-up. But there were still some scenes where we would have to maneuver and stop him in coordination with the moves and pauses of the humans in our cast.

"A cat can look at a king," is an old truism.

It is equally true that a cat can look at any person, and when he does he'll be looking up. If there were only a way of moving and positioning our signal above the heads of our people and out of camera, we would have a complete system of communication with D.C. He would respond to the high sound with accuracy, if we were skillful in making and using the equipment.

Obviously, the first step in solving the problem was to mount a speaker core on a pole. Art Vitarelli was working with me on the problem, and left the stage to see what equipment was available. He returned shortly with a long bamboo pole of small diameter. A speaker core was taped to one end of the pole, and a wire was spiraled around the pole from the core to the pole's lower end. The wire ended in a connector that could quickly be snapped into a lead from our console. A few wraps of tape snugged the wire to the pole.

"Let's try it," Art said.

It was a heavenly sound from far above the usual cameras's angle of acceptance. We knew D.C.'s acute hearing could tell the point of a sound's origin. Now we had to teach him to stop and look up at that point when he first heard the signal but not try to jump up at it.

Art lowered the pole to within a few inches of the floor, and I put a morsel of meat on the speaker core. On cue, D.C. left the trip box and went directly to the sound and the meat. Then he cocked his head and touched the pole as though impressed with the device. The next time I released the cat, Art held the core a couple of feet higher. D.C. stopped directly under it, then moved speculatively around beneath it, reared up and swung a paw at the sound he couldn't reach.

"Better dip in with the meat as soon as he stops," I told Art. "We've got to teach him that the sound, and sometimes the meat, will come to him each time he stops and looks up."

After a few more experiences, D.C. seemed convinced that if he stopped, looked up, and waited, the sound and a tidbit would come down to him. During a couple more training sessions, Art proceeded to raise the pole's end higher and lower it more slowly to the waiting cat. Art became very skillful at placing the sound so it would cause the cat to stop and wait on an exact spot. D.C. would show all the faith of the ancient Hebrews who waited for manna to fall from above.

Another technique in training had been discovered. Another problem had been solved. And another useful expression had been added to the working vocabulary of the crew of *That Darn Cat:*

"The principle of slowly descending manna."

Charlie,
The Lonesome Cougar

The Film's Story

Cougars had co-starring roles in several Disney films, but Disney Producer Winston Hibler decided it was time the cougar had a picture all its own.

The result was *Charlie, The Lonesome Cougar,* an outstanding animal adventure filmed in the rugged Pacific Northwest.

Raised from kittenhood by loggers, Charlie becomes something of a logger himself. When the time comes for him to return to nature, he finds it difficult to fend for himself because domesticity has dulled his instincts for survival. After his many lonesome vicissitudes, the forester who found him as a kitten takes Charlie to a wild-life refuge. There the cougar finds a mate to share his new life, and Charlie has finally come to the end of the lonesome trail.

Charlie, the Lonesome Cougar

For a change of pace, Bill Koehler's account from *Charlie* involved a mischievous raven in the film and a joke played on an unsuspecting camera man who tries to catch the bird. The moral to this story? Making Disney animal films is fun!

Actor Ron Brown feeds a hardboiled egg to Charlie.

"What do you want?"
Quoth the Raven

THE RAVEN that soared so gracefully against the blue sky of the Arizona high country was enjoying himself. The men who scowled up at him did not share his happiness. They were hungry. They needed only a few feet more of the raven on the ground and flying out through the pines to complete a sequence on *Charlie, The Lonesome Cougar,* before they could move to another location. And then they could eat lunch. But instead of coming back to earth for another take, the bird soared high above the frowns of the earthlings.

The man who owned the bird moved over to a sandy spot between two big rocks and squatted on his heels. He put his right hand close to his side and pawed the sand rhythmically with his fingers. "If you do this when he lands, he'll watch your fingers and you can get close and grab him. For about three times. Then he'll be wise to you and take off before you can grab."

"Is there any way you can get him back to earth so he can see you do that?" Ron Brown, the director on the unit asked.

"No," the raven's master said. "He won't come when I call him. But that's not because he's dumb. He can even talk."

The crew of four listened as a jeep ground its way up the steep grade to within a few hundred feet of the set.

"That'll be Herb Smith coming to see if we need anything," Ron said. He turned to the bird's owner. "Herb's a cameraman, but we've only been using one camera so far, so he's been a sort of handyman for us. What if Herb keeps track of the bird for us while we go back to the ranch for lunch?"

"It's okay with me," the man answered.

Herb Smith grinned as Ron explained the problem. "If he lands, should I try to catch him?"

The bird man nodded and went back to the sandy spot to demonstrate how to scratch the ground to arouse the bird's curiosity so he could be caught. "But remember, it'll only work about three times. After that he'll dodge you."

"Is that all I should know about him?" Herb asked.

"That's all. Just paw the ground," the bird man said.

The crew left for lunch, and Herb sat with his back against a big rock and stared up at the intense blue where he hoped the raven would appear. A jay, suspicious of any human who would sit so quietly, screamed and moved to a higher tree. Insects turned their metallic sounds on and off without giving away their locations. The fragrance that hot sunshine distills from dry vegetation and clear air made it a nice day to sit and watch.

Suddenly the raven appeared above an opening in the trees. He descended in tight spirals and landed on a dead limb of a ponderosa. Familiar with men, he was not alarmed by Herb's presence.

Herb waited quietly for the raven to come to earth. But the bird seemed content to study Herb from the dry limb. When Herb moved to the sandy place and made the recommended pawing in the sand, the raven watched with some interest, but moved only his head. Herb rose to his feet and moved casually to the tree.

The tree was young and less than a foot thick. Its bark was tight and smooth, and Herb was able to shinny quietly toward the lower limbs that started about ten feet up the trunk. He heard no sounds of flight and didn't raise his head until he slowly reached to grasp the lowest limb. He waited a moment then gripped another limb and eased himself a bit farther up the tree. He repeated the wait and move pattern until his head was on a level with the bird. He held a grip with his left hand and looked to one side of the raven as he raised his right hand for the grab. Slowly, he turned his head a bit more toward the bird to measure the distance for the final move.

"What do you want?" asked the raven.

The sounds of the insects ceased. A jay stopped his screaming. And Herb Smith was very quiet. Then, almost defensively, his hand flashed out and grasped the raven by the legs.

Without another word the bird resigned himself to being held as Herb carried him back to earth and placed him in his carrying cage.

Herb sat on a rock to rest. Every few minutes he turned to stare uneasily at the bird he had captured. He was still sitting when the crew returned from lunch. He showed no satisfaction when they saw the raven back in his carrier.

Hopefully, almost pleadingly, he asked: "Say, did you guys know that raven can talk?"

Sancho, the sled "dog."

Sancho,
The Homing Steer

The Film's Story

This heartwarming animal drama, based on a story by the famous Western writer J. Frank Dobie, appeared on the TV program, Walt Disney's Wonderful World of Color.

Sancho is a baby Texas longhorn steer, orphaned by the death of his mother and found by a kind rancher whose wife adopts Sancho as a pet. He soon grows to become a 1,500-pound steer and begins to cause all sorts of trouble around the ranch. So the rancher's wife turns Sancho over to her husband who takes the steer on the longest cattle drive in Texas. Sancho continues to give trouble and the rancher gives him to a pair of Indians to keep them from stampeding the herd.

Sancho devastates the Indians' camp and flees into the wilderness. Believing Sancho is safe, the rancher returns to the drive, never expecting to see the friendly steer again. But

Walt Disney and one of his biggest animal stars.

Sancho has different ideas and begins a 1,200-mile trek back to the ranch.

In his adventures, Sancho makes friends with a coyote that saves the steer's life, escapes from an attack by a pack of wolves and later meets a group of children who use him to pull their sleds. When one of the children's fathers decides to turn Sancho into steaks, the child frees the steer and shoos him away to safety.

Finally nearing his home, Sancho meets his final adversaries, a pair of mountain lions. The rancher appears on the scene and shoots one of the lions. Sancho drives off the remaining lion and he and the rancher return home together.

The Training

In the following two scenes from *Sancho* Bill Koehler first reports how his fellow trainer, Al Niemela, with the help of a visiting cowboy, "broke" Sancho to saddle and riding without the steer's gentle habit of pushing Al off with its long horn. Then ingenious Al invents a way to make 150 chickens roost in a tree in the bright mid-day sun against their natural habit of "going to bed" only when darkness falls.

Sancho saddled up for a ride.

How to "Break"
a Steer for Riding

THERE ARE TIMES when the action that an animal trainer believes will be the easiest to teach will prove to be the most difficult. When Al Niemela read the script for *Sancho, the Homing Steer,* he made notes on the things he would have to teach Sancho and the wolves and coyotes. Some of the patterns would be merely a matter of work and time, others would require a bit more ingenuity. The simplest thing should be to train Sancho to carry a rider on his back. Farm kids, from the days of the pioneers to the present have ridden milk cows, bulls and steers. Even the steers in rodeos have to be conditioned to buck. Al put the saddle sessions down at the bottom of his list of priorities.

Work with the wild animals was scheduled for the coolness of the mornings and evenings when the mood of the wolves and coyotes was most favorable to a good association with a man. Within a week, the wild creatures came to their gates in response to Al's voice, as eager for his affection as they were for the tidbits that he brought. He started an exacting program of building on their trust so that they were soon going to specific spots, stopping and doing other things that brought rewards.

Sancho got his schooling during the heat of the day. To the steer, being a domestic animal and separated from his kind, Al became his friend and the center of his world. The bond between Sancho and Al and the steer's exceptional intelligence permitted training to proceed rapidly. Very shortly, Sancho was moving to spots, lying down on cue and performing other routines reliably around various animals and distractions.

It was particularly hot on the day Al entered Sancho's corral with a saddle. The sun was reflected in the steer's coat as he bawled his usual welcome to Al.

"Look at the nice saddle I brought you," Al said, scratching at the root of Sancho's big ear.

Al spent several minutes talking to Sancho and patting the sleek hide. Then, without changing his tone, he tossed the girth over the broad back and settled the specially formed saddle in place. Sancho reacted no more than if a fly had landed on his back.

"See?" Al told him, "Sancho don't mind the saddle. Sancho's a good boy!"

The steer continued to stand quietly as Al reached under him and brought the girth's ring up to the cinch-strap. He tightened the cinch a bit. Sancho showed no resentment. Al left the saddle on the steer while he rehearsed the animal in some of the basic things he would have to do in the picture. Toward the end of the session, Al hung part of his weight on the side of the saddle. The steer showed no resentment.

"Good Sancho," Al said. "Tomorrow Al's going to ride you."

On the following day, Sancho stood calmly while Al hung

196

on the saddle and let his body press against the steer's side. Sancho had always been easy to lead and Al believed he would be somewhat responsive to the reins that were attached to his hackamore.

"Sancho's a good boy," Al crooned.

He patted the saddle and all of the sleek back he could reach, and his left hand locked the reins to the saddle horn. He continued the rhythmic patting until there was not the slightest reflex in Sancho's skin. Then he pulled himself up, swung a leg over the broad back, and waited.

Sancho stood quietly for a moment then casually swung his head around until a massive horn scraped Al from the saddle. There was no resentment, no hurry in the movement. It was as though Al's place was on the ground and Sancho meant to keep him there. Al remounted several times. The pattern was always the same: no bucking; no anger. He would scrape Al from the saddle, then stand, his brown eyes fixed on the face of his friend. Nor did the work on the many days that followed change the game of "mount and scrape."

Al began one day's session by tying Sancho close to a pine tree before he mounted him. The hackamore stopped his turn before Sancho's big head had moved a foot. Sancho rolled his eyes in Al's direction, but made no further movement as Al got off and on his back.

"Good Sancho," Al said as he led the steer from the tree. "I'll bet in three days you'll forget about pushing me off."

Four days later Al saddled Sancho and led him to the familiar tree, but did not tie him. Confident that the sameness of the situation would cause Sancho to stand as before, Al mounted. Immediately, a long horn came around and scraped him out of the saddle.

"Lead him up that hill."

Al turned around and recognized a rider from a nearby ranch. The cowboy twisted around in his saddle and pointed to the low hill that sloped sharply up from the corral.

"Why?" Al asked.

"So you can ride him down."

Al studied the hill. Erosion had cut its face into foot deep ridges, bared some of the larger stones, and set the smaller ones free on the steep surface.

"You can lead him, can't you?" the cowboy prompted.

"Sure. He follows that hackamore like it was his mother," Al said, "but what's the hill got to do with it?"

"When he comes down that hill, he'll be thinkin' so hard about placin' his feet, he won't have time to worry about what's on his back."

Al stared at the cowboy for a full minute, then shrugged his shoulders. He led Sancho to the hill, and he and the big steer began to work their way over ridges and loose rocks. There was a small flat area at the top that made it easy to turn the steer around and face him to the route they had climbed.

"Get him down on a rough place before you get on," the cowboy called.

Al stared at the man again, then led Sancho to where the steer was straddling one of the ridges. He coiled the lead-shank around the big neck, and took a long look at the slope.

"Get on," the cowboy yelled.

Al mounted as Sancho looked down at the footing that could take him from the uncomfortable hill; then, like a seasoned trail horse, he began to pick his way down the treacherous hillside. Twice he nearly slipped, but reached level ground without a fall; and went on into the corral.

"Good," the cowboy called as he headed his bay horse out through the scrub oak.

Al could understand how Sancho would be more con-cerned with what was under his feet than what was on his back when he was coming down a rough hillside, but why would one such experience influence him to ignore a rider on the level where the footing was good?

Al Niemela still wonders about that permanent impres-sion.

"Tying his head to a tree didn't do it. He'd go right back to scraping me off as soon as he could. Maybe it was his own decision on what to do when we came down that hill that changed his mind permanently. Whatever it was, he never tried to scrape me off again."

Getting the Fowls
to Roost in Broad Daylight

"IN THE DAYTIME?" Al Niemela asked. "You want the chickens to roost in that tree during the daytime?"

"They'll have to," the Director told him. "We have to shoot the scene day-for-night."

In a day-for-night shot, the camera's aperture is stopped down so small that the available light will produce only the faintest of images. The subject matter in the foreground is then illuminated with a bit of artificial light and will appear as objects seen at night and the unlighted background will reproduce so faintly as to enhance the illusion of darkness. The camera work is a matter of expertise. Al's task of getting the chickens to cooperate was without a job description, or even a precedent.

Al stood staring at the oak tree for several minutes after the Director walked away. Then he looked at the chickens, guinea hens and turkeys that scouted for insects among the rocks and cacti. There was nothing in the tree or the erratic movements of the chickens to offer a solution to his problem.

He went back to his project of training Sancho, "The Homing Steer," for his starring role, but his mind kept drifting back to the problem of turning poultry into day sleepers.

There was more challenge in the pea-brained fowls than in the fifteen-hundred-pound steer.

For several weeks, Al put in long days beneath the Arizona sun working with the big steer, and the wolves and coyotes that were part of his job. At such times when his work was mostly mechanical, and in any free time, his mind went to the problem of the day-roosting fowls.

One hot day Al finished a stint with Sancho and stood looking out toward the heat waves that blurred a distant mesa. He started to wipe his face with a big red bandana. He stopped suddenly as the bandana covered his eyes, and put it back in his pocket. Quickly he put Sancho in the corral, and headed for the shady side of a big rock where some chickens were dusting themselves. He trapped a hen against the rock and took it to his house trailer.

"Hold this chicken," he told his wife as he opened the door.

Ingrid Niemela is used to unusual requests, and held the hen very still while Al cut tiny strips of tape and placed one of them over each of the chicken's closed eyes.

"Now we'll find out," Al said, and headed out the door for the oak tree.

He gently placed the hen so her toes could close on a suitable limb, then watched her balance herself and settle comfortably into a roosting position. Now time would tell.

Two hours later the hen was still roosting contentedly, and as soon as the Director returned from scouting a location, Al called him to the tree.

"We've got our problem licked," Al told him. "You have the men catch the birds, and I'll mask their eyes. Then they can set them in the tree."

The following day, men clambered about the limbs of the

oak as though they were decorating a Christmas tree. Had a stranger chanced upon the sight of a hundred and fifty birds roosting quietly at mid-day, he would have doubted his sanity. If he had seen Sancho, the huge steer, walk into the scene and lie down at the foot of the tree as Al's melodious voice directed, he might have been more shaken.

To Al Niemela, the problem of the roosting poultry was solved. The challenge was gone. But soon there would be others.

The Bears and I

The Film's Story

When war veteran Bob Leslie, played by Patrick Wayne, ventures into the White Bird Wilderness to find the father of a deceased Army buddy, he becomes embroiled in a fight to preserve the heritage of a small Indian tribe whose way of life is threatened by governmental expediency and encroaching civilization.

At a settlement on the shores of White Bird Lake, Bob meets Chief Peter A-Tas-Ka-Nay, played by the real Indian Chief Dan George, who is the leader of the Bear Clan of the Taklute Tribe. The ex-soldier presents the Chief with the last of his son's belongings and tries in vain to comfort the proud Indian.

Bob decides to camp a while on the virgin forest setting and rents a cabin on the lake. One day he notices three bear cubs frolicking in a nearby meadow. He sneaks closer to get a better look. Suddenly, a large bear streaks from the under-

Wayne scans the trees looking for the person who shot Patch.

Patrick Wayne holds off a vicious dog who is trying to attack the bear cub.

Two of the cubs in *The Bears and I.*

brush and scares Bob to safety across a creek. The newcomer gets the mother bear's message: stay away from my youngsters.

Then tragedy strikes. Rifle fire breaks the silence of nature. Concerned for the safety of the bears he has grown fond of, Bob investigates. What he sees repulses him — the carcass of the mother bear.

At water's edge, Bob sees a trail of blood leading into the forest. He follows it and discovers the three terrified cubs perched high in a tree.

Bob adopts the lovable trio and takes them on hikes into the forest so that they won't become dependent on him, and they then learn to fend for themselves against a moose, a wolverine and a giant grizzly.

On one such trip, however, Bob makes the mistake of letting the bears accompany him to the Indian settlement. Members of the Bear Clan revere the animals as their brothers and are shocked to see the cubs on leashes. They tell Bob he must release them or evil will befall the Taklute Tribe. Despite Indian superstitions, Bob is determined to help the bears.

Finally, through Bob's efforts, the government permits the Indians to continue their life in the White Bird Wilderness as "Deputy Forest Rangers." And Bob reluctantly sets the bears free. He decides to finish college and become a ranger himself, hoping to return to the White Bird Wilderness and to the animals he loves.

The Training

Bill Koehler describes in the next two chapters the painstaking search Disney people made for the perfect natural setting for *The Bears and I,* and how Patrick Wayne and his family gave their unlimited cooperation to win the bears' affection so necessary to the success of the film.

Ron Brown Finds a Picture

SCOUTING FOR LOCATIONS can be a difficult job. One of the most grueling of such expeditions that Ron Brown has experienced began on the wall of Winston Hibler's office. The starting place was one of the sketches or "story boards" that described suitable locations for *The Bears and I.* The sketch, a work of art in itself, portrayed a wilderness lake against a background of snowy peaks.

Ron studied the picture for several minutes. "It's beautiful. Where is it?" he asked Winston Hibler.

"It's not from a photo," Hib said. "It's from the mind of the artist. But it suits us perfectly. We want you to find it—or one like it." He took the picture from the wall and handed it to Ron. "Go to Canada, but stay as close to the border as possible."

Ron covered hundreds of miles in British Columbia, binoculars in one hand and the sketch in the other. None of the beautiful places he saw had the appeal nor the potential usefulness of the concept from the artist's mind.

Usually, any location that is so remote it can be viewed only from the air is too inaccessible to be used by a full picture company of actors and technicians. What appears suitable from the air must be checked from the ground before decisions can be made.

But at last Ron felt the need for a plane to make a wider cast over the rough country. He was joined in his search by Bill Redland, the unit manager, and Bill agreed. The next day, a pilot in a float plane flew them over innumerable lakes, but none of them matched the ideal shoreline and background in the sketch.

Word came from the studio that a cast and crew had been selected, and a starting date for production had been scheduled. The finding of locations was now a race against time. Urgency prompted Ron and Bill to separate in their search. Ron would go farther north and probe the old logging and forestry roads. But Ron had more than his battered pickup truck. He had an idea.

Many miles north of where he had first scouted, Ron began his probing. Each time he chanced on a logging crew or a forester, or any kind of a settlement, he would jump out of his brush scarred pickup.

"Will you take a look at this?" was his stock question as he unrolled the sketch. "Have you ever seen a place that looks like this?"

Typically, there would be a period of study and a shake of the head. On some days there would be no lake country nor anyone to question; only narrow dead-end roads with holes that trapped his pickup until he could rescue it with his jack and armloads of brush.

"It began to seem as senseless," Ron recalls, "as walking around on the desert to find somebody who could tell you the nearest route to the Lost Dutchman Mine."

With the unreasoning faith that is part of any prospector, Ron decided to go still farther north.

It was two days later when on a one lane road he met another vehicle. The driver, in the green uniform of a forester, backed his Landrover to where he could ease off into some thin brush, and signaled Ron to pass. But instead, Ron left his pickup blocking the road and jumped out, with his sketch in hand.

"Oh," the forester said after a quick look, "that looks just like Chilikoot Lake. It's about fifty miles north of Williams Lake."

Carefully, Ron wrote directions in his notebook, and thanked the forester for the third time.

The next day Ron left the last of what could be described as a road and started on the trail that led to Lake Chilikoot. Twenty-seven miles of bumping and scraping brought him into a clearing at the lake's edge where a lodge and bunkhouses provided a facility for fly-in fishermen. Ron studied the scene. Somewhere along the lake's sixty-mile length there must be locations that would show the beauty of the setting to full advantage.

"The lake is big," Ron emphasizes, "and I figured a plane might save me some walking on the first survey, so I drove all the way back to the first phone, and called Bill Redland."

A float plane picked Ron up near the lodge the next morning, and soon he and the unit manager were scanning the shore as the pilot held the plane in slow flight about twenty-five feet above the water. Occasionally the pilot had to bank the plane as he followed the meandering shore and his two passengers would lose sight of land.

"It looks good from the air," Ron said above the sound of the plane. "Put me down near that point. I'll check things out from the ground as I walk back to the lodge."

A few minutes later Ron stepped from a pontoon into shallow water near the shore. He steadied the three cameras that hung around his neck as two more steps put him on dry

The beautiful site Ron Brown found for *The Bears and I*.

land. A few inches of late season snow crunched under his boots as he moved along the shore. Beauty was on every hand, but some of the scenes would require larger openings in the timber than any he could see. He walked on.

He came to a small rise about noon. Another sound blended with the breeze that shook snow from the trees and, as he topped the rise, Ron saw a stream. It flowed into the lake through a channel that was too deep to wade. He walked upstream to where the flow was wider and the water a little less swift. Somehow he had to cross the stream, and this could be the best place to try. He moved close to the bank and tried to estimate the depth of the water and the condition of the bottom, but the light from the murky sky did not penetrate the surface.

He placed his cameras on the stump of a windfall, which was roofed against the snow by the jagged end of its fallen trunk. There would be no risk to his cameras before he tried the footing. He removed all of his clothes, rolled them into a tight bundle, and tied them with his bootlaces. A slip could wet his clothes but he'd still have them. With the bundle over his head, he stepped from the snow into the water. The numbing cold reached to his shoulders by midstream, but then the bottom began to slope upward and he moved stiffly to within a few feet of the shore, and tossed his clothes up onto the bank. He headed back for his cameras and, empty handed and familiar with the bottom, crossed in half the time of the first passage.

His fingers were numb. Winding the camera straps around his hands to aid the grip of his numb fingers, he reentered the stream. His hands felt only the weight, not the form, of the cameras as he emerged from the water and laid them carefully in the snow beside his clothes. He swung his arms until his blue hands could brush some of the water from his skin. By the time his fingers and teeth had opened the knots on the bundle, most of the water had gone from his body and his violent shaking had subsided. He dressed, picked up the cameras and hurried on his way. A mile of brisk walking brought his body heat back to normal.

His course took him into a large open area that spread like a bay back from the edge of the lake.

Ron stopped abruptly. He took the sketch from his pocket and held it in his hands as he moved from one part of the clearing to another, photographing what he saw.

In his own words: "The shock of seeing that place made me forget about being cold and everything else. Within a block were all four major locations we would need for the picture, and all of them stood against that background of snow capped mountains. It looked exactly like the sketch."

He shot stills from every angle that Winston Hibler could possibly need, and then stood feasting on the grandeur around him. He was warm now. His job was done. Millions of Walt Disney fans would be thrilled by another authentic and beautiful background.

Bear Love

AL NIEMELA has worked with many kinds of animals, from chipmunks to grizzly bears. If you were to ask him to name a picture animal trainer's greatest asset, he would tell you that, on many pictures, it is an actor's unlimited cooperation.

"You can teach an animal to do many things, but you can't teach him to love someone," is Al's way of putting it. On some pictures this can be a concern that gnaws on a trainer night and day. Al felt such gnawing when he read the script for *The Bears and I*. Patrick Wayne would be the principal; and the bears, some of them small cubs, would have to interact directly with him. Al would not be close enough to give them any cues. The only way to assure the bears' right attitudes and actions would be through an affection for Pat.

Al shakes his head when he recalls his worries. "I spent part of my time working with the bears and ten other animals and the rest of it wondering how much cooperation I could expect from Patrick Wayne."

Give or take a few days, an actor joins a picture company when he is scheduled to appear before the camera. There would hardly be time for Pat and the bears to become acquainted with each other. Certainly, there would be no time to establish a real affection unless there would be unusual developments in weather or scheduling.

"It made me almost hope that we'd get a lot of rain before production and give Pat a little time to spend with the cubs," Al confesses.

Word came to the Olympic Game Farm that a tractor had finally opened the twenty-seven miles of a narrow road, allowing the company to move to its location in the Canadian wilderness.

"There wasn't any time to worry about anything else when we were getting our trucks and trailers over that road," Al recalls.

Al and his wife Ingrid, along with the rest of the company, finished their long day of bumping and scraping over the makeshift road, and pulled off into a clearing. They got out to join the others, who were enjoying the view of the lake and mountains. It was then that they were introduced to Patrick Wayne.

Al's blue eyes sparkle as he recalls the meeting. "We liked him right away. He's for real. The most genuine smile you ever saw. When he asked about the bears, I felt a ton lighter."

Pat's wife Peggy, and his children Michael and Melanie, rounded out a most attractive family, but it was natural for Al to wonder if after-work family activities would leave any spare time for the star of the picture to spend with the animals.

The bears were hardly in their new enclosures before Pat paid them his first visit. Al remembers that first meeting.

"His moves were just right, and he had a nice tone to his voice. Even the cubs seemed at ease with him, and he liked them, but he wasn't pushy. He knew it would take more time before he'd have their full confidence in every situation."

Pat spent a lot of time with the bears during the next few days. Often his wife and children would be with him. Al believed the bears were close to the point where they would respond to Pat even out on the sets.

"I knew if we could get in a week before production, we'd have it made. But it didn't work out that way. The director got ready in a hurry and the weather was good, so production started."

The first day, Pat worked in some scenes that had no bears. But even with simple scenes, the first day of production can be tiring. Most actors like to rest at the end of the day, or study their parts. Extra work is not welcome.

Summer days are very long in the Northland, and it was only dusk when Al started the bedtime check on his animals. The night was still, except for the sound of a few early night birds and the gentle lapping of waves from the lake shore. Then he heard something that seemed like a natural part of the night. They were the responsive sounds of bear cubs and human sounds expressing wholesome pleasure. In the late twilight, he saw the figures of Patrick Wayne and his family. Then through the sounds and silence of a family doing something together, came the words of little Michael Wayne:

"Good, baby bears."

As Al tells it: "Then I knew my worries were over. Those bears meant more to Pat than just something to work with. He enjoyed them. Somehow he'd find time to work with them."

Al was right. The family scene with the bears was repeated many times. By the time the bears went before the camera, they were as fond of Pat as they were of Al.

The gratitude is still in Al's voice as he tells fans: "Patrick Wayne is the finest actor to work with animals who's ever been in a Disney picture."

A real King!

King of the Grizzlies

The Film's Story

Seemingly, there is no film project that the Walt Disney nature photographers cannot tackle. And proof of this fact is the dramatic motion picture adventure feature, *King of the Grizzlies*. This thrilling story of one of the most feared and dangerous creatures that man has ever faced with a camera at close range was filmed against some of the most spectacular and breathtaking scenery of the Canadian Rockies, the grizzly's domain.

King of the Grizzlies is the moving tale of an Indian who sees represented in the great bear Wahb, all the power and wonder of nature. Forced to hunt down the animal who has been raiding the cattle of his rancher employer, the boy, Moki, is given an assignment he cannot bring himself to fulfill, for

Playing ''dead'' before the giant grizzly.

The ten-feet tall grizzly looks over the cattle situation.

there has developed a strong spiritual bond between the two. How this touching drama is resolved makes for one of the most exciting and colorful film stories ever produced.

This film is adapted from the book, "The Biography of a Grizzly," written by the famed nature author Ernest Thompson Seton, in the 1890's. But the giant bear and his habits have changed little since then, and few people fully understand or respect his immense size or power.

He is a wily beast that, when he rises on his hind feet, can walk like a man. The one in the picture stands ten feet tall and weighs over half a ton — some 1,300 pounds.

The Training

Bill Koehler recounted in an earlier chapter the lengths that Walt Disney Productions will go to find the ideal location for a wildlife film story. Here he tells about the huge task of getting the animal actors and film equipment up a snowbound mountain to the film site.

Herding the Bears
Up the Snow-clad Mountain

Fans often express their appreciation for the beauty and grandeur of the scenery in Walt Disney's wildlife productions. Their enthusiasm is shared by the crews that put in hours of hard work in those beautiful settings.

In the words of Lloyd Beebe: "One of the nice things about working for Disney's is that you're usually in a beautiful area that you enjoy."

Often the task of finding and using the best locations can be dramatic in itself. Getting there with the actors and equipment can be quite a job.

Beebe, who directed *King of the Grizzlies,* recalls one move to a location that is a good example of such difficulties. The production schedule called for a mother bear and her cubs to be filmed high on a mountain where the snow was giving ground to the green of spring. A few small patches of bare ground appeared in the upper areas that were exposed to direct sunlight but in most places the snow was still deep; and no trace could be seen of the one road that came near the location Lloyd had chosen.

Lloyd phoned Winston Hibler, Associate Producer on the picture, and explained the situation. "Hib" had time troubles of his own with the schedule and understood Lloyd's difficulties. They could wait a short time in hope that the road would soon be usable.

Lloyd went to the Highway Department and asked when they would be opening the road.

"It's not on our schedule yet," the supervisor told him. "We could get some more snow."

The week that followed was clear and cold. No more snow fell, but there was no noticeable thawing. Lloyd called the studio again, and was told there were time complications that would worsen if there was much more delay in getting to the location. Lloyd made several more trips to the Highway Maintenance Department. The answer was always the same.

"Don't know when we'll get to it."

The crew, the bears and equipment were ready. Only an open road that would put them within a reasonable distance of the location delayed their start.

On a bright afternoon Lloyd made a final call to the Maintenance Department, and learned there was still no date set to open the road. He called his crew together.

"We're not going to wait any longer," he told them. "We're going to start up there in the morning. Bring your snowshoes, sleeping bags and everything else you'll need."

Early the following morning two pickup trucks churned their way to where a winter's pack of snow had put a ten foot high wall between the lowlands and the forested slope of a mountain. Two men got out of each truck and began to stack the parts of heavy animal pens up on the bank of snow. They stepped into their showshoes, double checked their binders, then each slung a sleeping bag on his back. One at a time each man sidestepped his way up the steep bank and got a good grip on the shelter parts. Then, with Lloyd choosing the course, the men began to zig-zag their way up the mountain. The loads were heavy and the rest stops grew more frequent and longer. In the early afternoon a cold wind blew across the snow but it didn't dry the sweat on the faces of the men as they worked their way up the steep slopes. It was dark when the crew reached a flat close to the location and dropped their loads beneath a big fir.

Two weeks passed before all of the equipment and supplies had been carried up the mountain. Now only the bears were needed to start production.

"We should start at dawn when we bring the bears up," Lloyd told his men. "I don't want to run out of light before we get to the top."

There was a small patch of gray in the east when the mother bear and her two cubs were unloaded at the snow bank. Then began one of the most strenuous and comical leading, herding and shoving programs ever seen on any mountain. The mother was willing to be led as long as the cubs followed close to her. The cubs seemed to want to follow the trail left by their mother and the man who led her, except when the space between themselves and the men who herded from behind widened; then they would veer off on their own, barely able to break a trail through the unmarked snow. Then a flanker on showshoes would bend to the job of turning the runaways back to the procession. During each of these excursions, the mother would sit down and bawl, and the man with the lead shank would have to wait until the two others could shove her into motion again. This concentration on the mother would often give the cubs another chance to clown around on their own, at which time the flanker would turn them back and the mother would be willing to move onward and upward.

Darkness was but a few minutes away when the procession

reached the spot where the pens had been reassembled, near the place where the first scene would be shot.

One of the men fed the hungry bears while another started cooking a quick meal for the crew. Within an hour the men were in their sleeping bags.

"Listen," Lloyd said during the second day of production. "Over toward the road."

The sound was that of a heavy engine, muffled by the snow. The telltale exhaust ran up and down the scale from slow idling to a massive effort.

From the high point where they stood the crew and the three bears looked down to where plumes of snow were flying into the air.

"Oh, no!" Lloyd said.

A few hundred yards from where they stood, the men saw a giant snowplow.

"The road's open," Lloyd said softly.

The Ugly Dachshund and his "littermates."

The Ugly Dachshund

The Film's Story

This rollicking story, based on a popular novel by G. B. Stern, teams up a pair of newly-weds who try to cope with a group of canine cut-ups in a vain attempt to preserve tranquility in their happy home.

When a Great Dane puppy grows up with a litter of Dachshunds and believes himself to be one of the smaller breed, the hilarious results shouldn't happen to a dog — much less, people.

The young husband Mark Garrison, an artist played by Dean Jones, is awakened by his attractive wife Fran, played by Suzanne Pleshette. She tells him, "The time is now. We'd better get to the hospital." Dressing hurriedly, Mark calls the doctor and they dash for their car.

Speeding along the highway, they are stopped by a police officer, but when he thinks he detects the emergency of their plight, he provides a motorcycle escort to the nearest hospital. As the officer dismounts, he is startled to see the Garrisons speeding away in the opposite direction. He chases them. He catches up with them at the veterinary hospital as Fran rushes her expectant Dachshund in for delivery. Mark is confronted by the irate policeman who feels he has been badly misled. Mark gets a ticket.

Dr. Pruitt, the veterinarian played by Charlie Ruggles, soon announces that Danke has given birth to three puppies and mother and daughters are doing fine. He suggests the Garrisons stay overnight, just to get the puppies off to a good start.

The next day Mark goes to the veterinarian to pick up Danke and her litter. Dr. Pruitt persuades him to take along a Great Dane puppy that has been cast out by its mother.

Mark arrives home with Danke and *four* puppies. Fran thinks Danke has given birth to another puppy and happily ignores its difference in size and appearance.

As the awkward puppy begins to outgrow his nursery mates, the truth becomes painfully obvious. Brutus, as he has been named, is a very great Great Dane.

Thus begins a confusing time for Brutus. The only dogs he ever sees are Danke and her puppies. He comes to the conclusion that he too is a Dachshund. He follows the little dogs around and tries to mimic everything they do. He even learns to walk in a sort of slouch so he will be small like a Dachshund. But no matter how low he slouches, Brutus is still enormous. His size and clumsiness get him into all sorts of trouble. He tries to explore Mark's studio and, quite by accident, wrecks the place.

Suzanne Pleshette and one of the Dachsie puppies.

The Dachshunds love to frolic on Fran's bed but when Brutus joins them, the bed collapses. Only poor Brutus is found out and blamed.

Fran and Mark plan a garden party. After the guests arrive, Chloe, one of Danke's puppies, gets into the yard where Brutus is tied up. She teases the big dog by gnawing a bone right in front of him. Brutus tears loose and chases little Chloe through the party. It is chaos. Brutus knocks down one of the caterers. A whipped cream cake is sent splattering all over everything. The buffet is ruined. In the melee, guests take refuge on a bridge spanning a lily pond. The bridge promptly collapses and dumps everyone into the water.

Mark decides Brutus must learn he is *not* a Dachshund, but a Great Dane. He begins training the dog for the show ring but keeps it a secret from Fran, who is training Chloe for the coming dog show too. Brutus responds well to the training, except for one thing. He lacks the proud, self-assured look of the Great Dane. It's the Dachshund influence. Brutus still stoops and slouches a little.

Show time arrives. Mark and Dr. Pruitt slip Brutus into the show tent without Fran's knowledge. Brutus does very well in competition with the other Great Danes until a woman carrying a Dachshund stops near the ring. Brutus sees the Dachshund and immediately slouches into his "Dachsie" walk.

The judge asks sharply if the dog is ill. It seems that Brutus will surely be disqualified. Then a beautiful harlequin Dane appears with her handler. Like all males who try to show off in the presence of a lady, Brutus straightens up and assumes his proudest stance. He is every inch a Great Dane and walks off with the blue ribbon.

Meanwhile, poor Fran has shown Chloe, who comes out only second best. When Mark learns this, he hides Brutus's blue ribbon to avoid hurting Fran. But she sees Brutus in the ring with Dr. Pruitt, competing for best of winners. To Mark's delight Fran isn't angry. She is proud of Brutus, too, and of Mark. What's more, she decides to give up dog shows, blue ribbons and all such snobbish, doggy nonsense. She and Mark will work together, make a good home, and if they raise dogs at all they'll be strictly for pets.

The Training

In the following account, Bill Koehler tells how he and his associates overcame the problems of training very young puppies for their roles in the picture. Young puppies want only to do their own things, like eating and playing. How Bill and his partners got the puppies to perform like seasoned troupers and become five most appealing dog stars is as funny and fascinating as the movie itself.

Time to get up!

Chaos in the studio.

The Dachsie Demolition Team

IT'S A DIM EYE that's not attracted to a puppy and a cold heart that doesn't open to the one baby animal, above all others, that is a bearer of so many good things from God to mankind.

Dachshund puppies are particularly hard to resist. Their comical stature and purposeful expressions and generally winsome ways are entrancing. But as we selected the pups who would be candidates for roles in *The Ugly Dachshund,* our enchantment was tempered by what we had read in the screenplay. The pups would have to do more than be charming. They had to do many things. They had to be competitive and mischievous. At the moment, the eight we had selected were not competitive and mischievous. They were quizzical as they stood or sat in a group and frowned up at us, as though asking why we didn't do something. The look we focused down on them was equally quizzical as we wondered how we were going to get them to do the difficult things the script demanded.

The two sets of pups that would do the most work were about seven weeks old at the time. They would be only a few weeks older when the production started. Some of the action they faced would be difficult for mature, trained dogs.

And they seemed too young for serious training. Using

bait or bribery to get the difficult actions, such as carrying and entangling balls of yarn, would be a weak motivation for animals that are working at liberty and exposed to the free choice of distractions on a big stage. To depend on puppy play would be impossible too. Puppies doing cute things of their own choice, when they wanted to, would have no value to our picture. We needed pivotal actions to make story points.

"One thing's certain," my partner, Hal Driscoll, said, "they're probably too young to take any serious training. They're interested in two things—eating and playing."

"That's for sure," agreed J.R. Randall, one of our staff who would do most of the work with the pups. "We need exact things at exact places—and at exact times."

"And bait's out," Hal put in, with the contempt that a good trainer has for food bribery. He seemed to shudder at the thought of trying to work several pups simultaneously in a shot with nothing stronger than food rewards.

We stood quietly in the coolness of Stage 4, exchanging stares with the eight shiny pixies on whom so much depended. We were casting about for breed characteristics that could be used to motivate the puppies. The others listened while I reviewed the history of the breed.

"Back in the Dachsie's busiest working days he was more of a terrier than he was a hound. He fought varmints underground, when they holed up ahead of other hounds. Dachsies were not competitive with each other; in fact, they would take turns digging. One or two would rest outside a den while another dug. They seemed content to let other hounds do the hunting and chasing. They did the digging and fighting."

J. R. Randall is an attentive listener. He had been weighing all the facts as I reviewed the Dachshund's origin and purpose.

"Anything in that background that will help you?" I asked him.

"Could be," J.R. answered. "Let me just play around with them for a while before we start a program."

In addition to his work with the little Dachsies, J.R. would work with some Great Dane pups, and a young adult Dane. Gretchen, our well trained Dachshund would play the part of the mother. Duke, our Great Dane from *The Swiss Family Robinson* and other pictures, would do the more difficult parts of the mature Ugly Dachshund.

My partner and I would be working on other pictures and would be training with J.R. only occasionally.

"We'll need to get them used to the stage in a hurry," J.R. said, "So I'll do all of the work here. I'll just haul them back and forth from the kennel every day."

The Dachshund pups changed a great deal within the next few days. They followed J.R. around the big sound stage, "discovering" a multitude of sights, sounds and smells. In turn, an individual pup would stop to probe something with an inquisitive nose, then streak to catch up like a shiny torpedo. Office employees, on their customary noon walk around the lot, stopped by the stage to visit the beguiling little characters who reared up against the wire of their big exercise pen. All this experience helped to convince the pups that they owned a world filled with intriguing things and people who wished them well. Within ten days the pups were at home on the stage.

Because of their age, J.R.'s progress with the pups came more through his ingenuity than their trainability. "How can you tell them apart?" he was often asked. "They all look alike."

"It's easy," he would answer. Differences in reactions and expressions made each pup an individual to him. They quickly learned the names he gave them, and each responded with curiosity to squeakers, and would rush to see a pet white rat in a cage. Because a bell could be concealed in various target areas on a set, J.R. taught them to charge wildly to where a bell signal promised a peek at the rat or some other delightful surprise. Fortunately, they would seldom have to stay still unless they were naturally occupied with some sight or sound, so there was no need to try to teach them solid stay positions.

Because I was working on another picture nearby, I had the opportunity to make several visits each day to J.R.'s "training camp" in the seclusion of the big stage and observe the progress the pups were making under his gentle pressure. At the end of a long day, I stopped by to watch him give the pups "one more lesson" in holding lengths of yarn in their mouths until he took it from them and gave each a small tidbit.

"They're doing pretty well on most things," J.R. said as he looked from one to another of the pups who seemed ready to be loaded into the truck for the trip to the kennel. "But their attention span is still awfully short, and in those big carrying scenes they'll need to hold things for a long time. No reward is going to make them concentrate long enough. I've got to come up with something else."

When he was an outstanding football player, J.R.'s face would freeze in a slight frown that showed a lot of determination. He was wearing that frown as he talked. I felt he'd get those pups to concentrate longer, but I didn't know how. The next day as I rushed from the set where I was working to get some equipment from my van, I saw J.R. go through the big door of Stage 4 with a long carpet tube balanced on his shoulder.

Two days later I had my first chance to again visit J.R.'s puppy project. The carpet tube had been painted white. It had been placed among his complex of equipment, its ends were cradled by short boards with cleats to keep it from rolling.

"Hold this pup," J.R. said by way of greeting. "Hold him so his head is starting inside the tube."

The pup squirmed eagerly when J.R. squeaked a rubber rat at the far end of the tube. The muffled sound of the squeaker ignited the pup. He shot out of my grip and hurtled through the tube. The frantic scratch of his nails marked his progress. Then came the faster squeaks of the badly bitten "rat." J.R.'s arm shook as the pup fought to tear the toy from his hand. He let the pup win after a brief tussle, and blocked the tube end with his knee. Now the sounds and vibrations changed course as the pup backed out of the tube. A wagging tail emerged, followed by a sleek body, then the head, locked firmly on the toy rat, cleared the pipe.

Considerable time elapsed while the pup drew the toy rat from the tube.

"How many of them will stay with a job that long?" I asked.

"Four of the eight," he told me. "They seem to get more fired up each time I work them. They figure anything they drag out of that tube is a real varmint. It's like they really caught something and they want to hang onto it."

"Do you think you can transfer the attitude to carrying other objects, even when they don't pull them out of the tube?" I asked.

J.R. weighed the question. "I don't know if I can get it done by the time we start production." He looked around at the eight pups. "Possibly, if I have help so I can double the time I put on them, and still put enough work on the grown dogs."

The next day the studio gave a call to Corky Randall, J.R.'s brother. Corky, like J.R., had grown up with animals and had the savvy and coordination to help with both the puppies and the grown dogs. The two started a crash program of work. Early and late. Although I had early calls on the set where I worked, J.R.'s truck would be parked outside Stage 4 when I arrived. Often they would be still training and rehearsing when I finished work at night.

Because some of the most important parts of *The Ugly Dachshund* were the demolition scenes where the Dachsies and the Dane caused chaos, much of the training and rehearsal consisted of having the dogs pull, tear, carry and trample a variety of things over catwalks and obstacles to prepare them for the assaults on Dean Jones' studio and Suzanne Pleshette's living room.

One evening I went to Stage 4 to check on the progress. I watched three Dachshund pups rip a cloth apart and then scramble away in different directions, heads high and bearing their trophies like victory flags. J.R. made a yipping sound and the pups followed him back to their big exercise pen. Next, Corky Randall brought in Diego, one of our Dane doubles, and fastened an extra long leash to the dog's wide collar. He tied the other end to the axle of an old baby carriage. He stayed with the dog and buggy while J.R. took a position on the far side of the stage. On J.R.'s call, Diego streaked forward. The buggy sideswiped the leg on a table, and the buggy tipped on its side and slid along without slowing the big dog in the slightest.

"He'll jerk that serving cart right through anything that gets in his way in the big lawn party riot," J.R. said as he brought the Dane and the sliding buggy back toward us. "Let's put Diego away. Then we'll run the pups once more on the obstacle course before we quit for the night."

The catwalks consisted of narrow planks that formed

236

inclines between boxes that varied in height. As each of the four pups was placed on the catwalk and given his little ball of yarn, he carried it the length of the course and down the last sloping board to the floor. From the Dachshund pups to the Dane who was The Ugly Dachshund, the dogs seemed almost ready to create controlled chaos.

The interior sets for *The Ugly Dachshund* were built on a stage adjacent to the one where J.R. and Corky trained and rehearsed the pups. Because it was an important story point that the dogs would wreak havoc on the expensively furnished rooms, it was not possible to rehearse on the sets after they were dressed. In spite of J.R.'s tremendous effort, the pups would still enter the world of the dressed and lighted sets as untried actors. Our cast included pups of various sizes, both Great Danes and Dachshunds, and some adult dogs of each breed that were experienced performers. The half grown Dachsies had to do many things that would be blamed on the Danes so we reasoned that our problems would be with them.

The picture I was working on was completed a few days before production on *The Ugly Dachshund* was due to start, and I was able to join J.R. and Corky for the pups' baptism of lights and confusion. Along with their mother, our four best Dachsie pups and the Dane that had outgrown his "family" were shown in the lavish settings they would later destroy. In this edited picture these scenes would follow the sequences that showed the newborn litter, among which a sympathetic Dean Jones had added the orphaned Dane puppy.

We got off to a good start. The pups seemed to feel that the whole affair was staged so the crew and others could show them attention. Dean Jones and Suzanne Pleshette put a warmth into their relationship with the dogs that would make the story truly believable, so the pups were at ease and the establishing shots went smoothly. But on the morning we faced the first of the vandalism scenes, we knew that a real test would begin. Four Dachsies and a young Dane would have to work in coordination and in maniacal fury.

Prayerfully we crouched on the sidelines and sent them into battle. It was awesome. Four missiles shot out onto the floor of Dean's studio and grabbed at paintings, papers, and brushes. At times, as though destroying a masterpiece, they teamed up and turned a hapless painting into a jig-saw puzzle in a few seconds. The young Dane knocked a steady supply of new challenges from the shelves and tables for them. They climbed to more accessible places and slid down the backs of furniture like otters. The room was sufficiently vandalized to provide a believable shock to Dean and Suzanne when they came home.

Next on the list of targets were the tastefully appointed living room and den. The decor was quickly changed when the Dachsies enmeshed all the furnishings with ball after ball of Suzanne's yarn and the great lengths they unraveled from a nearly completed sweater. Their stillness, born of exhaustion, gave them the look of innocence, and as usual Suzanne's wrath was visited on Dean and his Dane.

There was no letdown in the vandals' competitiveness in the big scene of "the garden party." Dozens of excitable guests furnished a perfect course for the wild scuttling of the Dachsies and the Great Dane to snag his leash on a serving cart and drag it, bearing a rider, through the melée. It was wild. Whether the pups were carrying, pulling or just running they seemed constantly fired by the competitive spirit that J.R.'s long days had developed in them.

At last the party was over. Dean and Suzanne were left with the shambles and no guests.

Those of us who had worked with the dogs were left with the mixed feelings of a job well done and a new problem. The combination of pack instinct and competitiveness that gave the pups their drive and tenacity when they locked onto things and ran could cause trouble in the shot where four pups were to make peace with Dean by bringing him gifts. It might be quite a job to slow them and get them to drop their presents at Dean's feet.

A long "brainstorming session" with the Randalls, my partner Hal, and me produced a single idea. Maybe we could make the spirit of competition that was our problem work for us.

That evening we took the pups over to Stage 4, lifted one of the most aggressive ones from the crate and gave it to Corky to hold. He took a rubber rat from a box of toys and tossed it a few feet in front of the pup. The pup struggled in Corky's hands.

"Let him go," J.R. said.

The pup's busy jaw brought squeaks from the rat as he ran in a circle on the big stage. J.R. took a piece of fur from the box and tied a string on it. He tossed it out toward the closest point of the pup's circle, and gave the string a little tug when the Dachsie made the next round. The pup, rat still in his mouth, stopped and looked at the twitching fur, then was off on another circle.

"Get another pup out," J.R. said.

As the second pup was faced toward the fur, J.R. tugged on the string. Again the pup with the rat circled back. He stopped again when he saw the fur, but this time, before he could start another circle, the second pup streaked out and grabbed the fur.

The "circler" dropped the rat and in a moment was

helping to stretch our fur that felt much more like a varmint than did the rubber rat. Further trials showed that the fur had a stronger appeal to all of the pups than any other toys did.

"They'll trade whatever they're carrying for that hunk of fur," J.R. said. "Now if we can associate a sound cue with the fur to attract their attention, we should be able to get them to stop and release those presents."

For three days, between shots and after production hours, J.R. and Corky worked on the pups. Hal and I were busy with shots that featured the Danes, and saw little of the puppy training. Then the daily call sheet showed we would open in the den set the next morning.

We checked the lights to see where we could position ourselves; and breathed easier when we saw that J.R. and Corky would be directly in line with the pups and the spot where they should stop. There were no lights directly behind them, so they would cast no shadows into camera and the pups would not be blinded as they came through the dining room door.

Our Director, Norman Tokar, explained the action. There would be an establishing shot of the room, showing Dean Jones in a chair. Then the pups, one at a time, would enter, stop on a spot at Dean's feet, drop his gift, and look up.

While the Randalls took their positions in the den, Hal and I, with some help from a prop man, would hand the pups their presents and release them from out of sight in the living room when J.R. rang his bell.

I gave the first pup his gift when the camera operator said "speed" and released him on the sound of J.R.'s signal.

We knew the pup had made it to his spot when we heard J.R. thump the floor, the pup's cue to drop his present and look for the fur. Although we couldn't see it happen from our positions we could visualize J.R. holding the fur for the pups to look up. The pattern was repeated with the other three pups.

Then we heard the word "Cut," and walked into the den. We saw smiles that matched J.R.'s terse, "It looked good."

We put the pups back in their exercise pen, and relaxed with a cup of coffee while we watched them mill about, their foreheads wrinkled as though they were trying to think of some new game.

"You guys sure put it into them," I told J.R. "I guess there's nothing like competition for people or puppies."

J.R. nodded. "Competition's a good motivation. But I'll tell you one thing," he paused for a moment and went on, "Looking back over those long days, I learned competition doesn't always mean free enterprise."

Lloyd Beebe, the creator of the Olympic Game Farm, and a newborn cougar.

The Olympic Game Farm

*The paradise where Disney
animals go between the acts*

IT IS INTERESTING to know how well Disney fans remember the wild animals that have appeared in Disney Productions. Their interest and affection are expressed in many questions.

"What happens to the animals when a picture is finished? Are they simply put back in cages?"—are two concerns the fans have about their animal friends.

The Olympic Game Farm is the answer. It is a gratifying answer to those who have met the animals through Disney pictures and who love wildlife and are interested in its preservation.

A tour through the Olympic Game Farm is most rewarding when you know something of the character and goals of Lloyd Beebe, the man who conceived and, with the personal encouragement of Walt Disney, brought his concept to life.

Lloyd has associated closely with a variety of wild creatures from the Antarctic through the magnificent wilds of Canada. His knowledge of wild things and their environment has made him concerned with their preservation. He was one of the first to sense the need to propagate some endangered species in a

Welcome to our farm!

Catherine Beebe and a friend.

farm situation for restocking an environment that chance had injured or depleted. As nearly as possible he wanted his animals to feel some of the pleasures they would enjoy in the wild: unpolluted air, pure water, and sights and sounds that would be more interesting than any zoo type concept could supply.

In the cases of grazing animals, the lush fields at his own farm were a ready answer. However, such creatures as tigers, cougars, wolves and bears were a different matter. But Lloyd was determined that his big cats and other carnivores would not spend their time caged on concrete where they would see, hear and smell only man made things.

The land where he would create the Olympic Game Farm was located on the Olympic Peninsula near Sequim, Washington. The breezes that move across the area carry a combination of wood and water scent that is unique to the area. Lloyd's bountiful wells ran water that was pure and sweet. There was the perpetual green of firs, cedars and lesser vegetation. Because the drainage was so good, Lloyd could build the kind of facilities he wanted for his carnivores.

Men and equipment began work on the runs. Instead of slabs of concrete, wire was set below the surface of the ground and then the earth was replaced. As soon as the big runs and sleeping areas were completed, the run surfaces were covered deeply with fragrant fir bark that was absorbent and could constantly be replaced.

A tiger was the first animal to inhabit the new runs. Before Lloyd had acquired him, the big cat had lived on concrete. Lloyd watched unobtrusively from a distance and could feel the cat's satisfaction as he walked back and forth on naturalness of the springy bark. Grass grew against the end of the run. Then the tiger crouched at the end of the run and sniffed at

The buffalo still roam at Olympic Game Farm.

It's a long way from Africa, but the grass is good.

Al Niemala and friends go for a hike along the creek.

One of the Olympic Game Farm's big polar bears.

the grass that grew against the wire. He turned and stretched, and the flexing of his toes drove his claws deeply into the bark.

Lloyd smiled knowingly as the beautiful creature looked across the field of grazing animals and toward the Olympic Mountains. Some tame Canada geese and mallards meandered by in the sociable way of waterfowl, and the tiger watched it all with the calm interest that is the attitude of wild animals when they feel no hunger.

Lloyd saw the same reaction each time another animal entered the new quarters. The animals were contented in their comfortable and interesting environment. Now Lloyd could get on with some other innovations.

You have probably been thrilled by the performance of a great wild animal act. The reliability and unvarying precision are a testimony to a trainer's ability. But it is this absolute adherence to a routine and rhythm that would make the performing animals unsuited to motion picture acting. Lloyd Beebe knew that the same thing could be said of those wild animals that are rigidly trained to act or react in a specific way for a scene. If the scene had to be altered, as is often the case, or if other scenes called for different reactions to a similar atmosphere, such animals are confused and almost useless. One over-stressed experience could make a potentially versatile animal a "one shot actor." Lloyd would use a better way of motivating animals so that there would be no experiences to cause them to be confused on later pictures. He shared his philosophy with those on his staff.

In his words: "The animals must be very friendly to you. I'd rather have a man who can tame an animal than a man who can train one. Someone who can raise an animal that trusts him and keeps on trusting him is Number One to me. Such an animal is more apt to look like he's doing things on his own."

248

The staff of the Olympic Game Farm would spend time in association with their animals. The association would be without carelessness, ever mindful that the animals were wild. The men involved must be constantly aware of how their actions would appear to the animals. Even after the "feel" for an animal was acquired, actions of the staff, outside as well as inside the enclosures, would be unobtrusive, never "pushy" nor over-confident.

Out on location Lloyd's precepts are followed with equal care: "I don't like any rough business. There are ways of getting it without that. We don't do things to spoil them. If an animal has confidence in you, you can arrange his environment for a scene so he'll do what you want in a natural way.

A vital part of an animal actor's value is in his appearance. He must be kept in top condition, so that he will feel, look and act well. A viewer's own observation of an animal will disprove the lie that they are fasted and kept underweight so that they can be "baited" from one point to another. Unfortunately there are some kind folks who are distressed when they read sensational articles by writers who are ridiculously illogical.

In some picture animal establishments, a rush to meet a production date, and other exigencies, will often interrupt a carefully planned program of rearing and taming animals. Lloyd uses an exquisitely simple principle to prevent such sacrifices at the Olympic Game Farm.

"Work bare-handed when you're handling an animal and your moves will be better. To put on heavy gloves and then grab a young animal for any reason, even if you're in a hurry, is a sure way to lose his confidence. The one that's been spooked by a 'gloved grabber,' whose moves and mind are bad, is not an animal that you can depend on to work confidently with an actor."

Cute cougar cub at the farm. Its spots will disappear as it matures.

Lloyd Beebe and Joey, the wolverine.

Well, hello there!

A proud mother and the first moose calf born at the Olympic Game Farm.

The trust that Lloyd's animals have in their handlers is evident during travel and work in the strangeness of distant sets. Lloyd and his men have a constant awareness of how their animals will react to the environment in which they are placed. They know how to do little things to the environment that will cause an animal to act predictably and naturally in the way the scene requires—in the last scene of a picture as well as the first.

Most gratifying of all to the fans who love our Disney animals, when his work on a picture is finished, an animal is not put back in a close confinement and forgotten. He is returned to the comfortable and cheerful Olympic Game Farm, where the staff continues the program of keeping him confident and happy.

These happy homecomings from a job well done are individual tributes to Walt Disney.

A goal has been reached by Lloyd Beebe. It's his pleasure to share his love of animals with the thousand of Disney fans who tour the Olympic Game Farm. He's proud that they will find their animal friends cared for in the Walt Disney tradition.